TWENTY POEMS
THAT COULD SAVE AMERICA

and Other Essays

Also by Tony Hoagland

POETRY

> *Unincorporated Persons in the Late Honda Dynasty*
> *What Narcissism Means to Me*
> *Donkey Gospel*
> *Sweet Ruin*

ESSAYS

> *Real Sofistikashun: Essays on Poetry and Craft*

TWENTY POEMS
THAT COULD SAVE AMERICA

and Other Essays

Tony Hoagland

GRAYWOLF PRESS

This publication is made possible, in part, by the voters of Minnesota through a Minnesota State Arts Board Operating Support grant, thanks to a legislative appropriation from the arts and cultural heritage fund, and through grants from the National Endowment for the Arts and the Wells Fargo Foundation Minnesota. Significant support has also been provided by Target, the McKnight Foundation, Amazon.com, and other generous contributions from foundations, corporations, and individuals. To these organizations and individuals we offer our heartfelt thanks.

Published by Graywolf Press
250 Third Avenue North, Suite 600
Minneapolis, Minnesota 55401

www.graywolfpress.org

Published in the United States of America

ISBN 978-1-55597-694-1

2 4 6 8 9 7 5 3 1
First Graywolf Printing, 2014

Library of Congress Control Number: 2014935837

Cover design: Jeenee Lee Design

Cover photograph: Garry Winogrand, *New York,* ca. 1963.
© The Estate of Garry Winogrand, courtesy Fraenkel Gallery, San Francisco.

*Dedicated to my colleagues and friends
of the Warren Wilson community*

CONTENTS

PREFACE

American poetry in the twenty-first century is a diaspora of aesthetic camps and dispositions so diverse as to defy generalizations. Even so, this book begins with a generalist essay on American poetic diction, and it ends with a broad exhortation for poetry's relevance and vitality in our country's school systems. In between, not so hidden among other appreciations and critiques, I find, to my own surprise, a recurring complaint about the lack of adulthood represented in much new American poetry. The presence of this theme surprises me because I am an ardent believer in poetical irreverence, spontaneity, informality, and subversion of decorum—qualities not usually associated with maturity.

Though it was not a conscious agenda in writing these essays, I nonetheless stand by my complaint. I believe that poetry has a role to play in contemporary American culture, and that it has lately retreated from that risk, that faith, and that opportunity. Much contemporary poetry seems written with a dim and anxious awareness of its marginal status in American culture, but the result, paradoxically, has been an increase in our overall aesthetic insularity. Meanwhile, the avant-garde continues to make its dubious claims of political credentials; the uber-theorists and technicians create their Rubik's cubes of difficulty; and the charming but superficial disco-dance of Personality has crowded into the verbal foreground of many poems, displacing the enterprise of sustained thought, emotional intensity, ethical agency, and even subject matter itself.

"From the place where we are right," says the Israeli poet Yehuda Amichai, "Flowers will never grow," by which he means, truly, that

self-righteousness is sterile. One should know better than to preach. ✓
The essays here praise poetry more than they chastise, and they embrace a broad range of the American poetic spectrum. I hope that my attempts at understanding, my voice, and even my prejudices stake out one useful position in the complex conversation of this moment.

T. H.

Olit
4/19

TWENTY POEMS
THAT COULD SAVE AMERICA

and Other Essays

◇ ◇ ◇ ◇ ◇

Je Suis ein Americano:
The Genius of American Diction

We American poets are millionaires; we possess a vocabulary extracted, imported, and patched together from so many tongues and sources, we can write checks with our mouths all day. We inhabit a linguistic landscape so etymologically wealthy that our most minor communications are studded with high and low improvisations. We have *tinhorn* and *yahoo* and *meshuganah*; we have *yonder* and *redneck* and *hokeypokey*, we have *lily-livered* and *bumbershoot* and *rockabilly.* Our diction is already mixed—a mixture of nationalities, jargons, eras, and attitudes. "The English language," said Whitman, "is the accretion and growth of every dialect, race, and range of time. . . . It is indeed a sort of universal absorber, combiner, and conqueror."

The receptivity of English to creative mongrelization may spring from its hybrid origins—from the Norman Conquest, in 1066, when Anglo-Saxon met French-Latin, and Middle English was conceived. Our forked tongue thus includes both *work* and *labor,* both *dead* and *mortified,* both *hungry* and *famished.* As a result perhaps, English, and especially American English, seems never to have taken a puritanical stance toward vocabulary. It has enlarged itself by freely absorbing vocabulary from Arabic, Iroquoian, and Indonesian. Other countries, such as France, have striven to shield and protect the purity of their language. But Americans love coinages and improvisation—linguistically, we don't mind being "balkanized."

In consequence, English is fantastically elastic and adroit. We possess so many alternative options for naming that our available expressive range is vast. Each synonym carries different implications, or connotations, of relative high and low, of attitude, formality, distance, and inflection. Thus, a poet can "say the same thing" on a semantic level while spinning the message in any variety of ways: *pregnant* is also *knocked-up, gravid, expecting, bun in the oven, one on the way, great with child,* and so on and so on.

Few poems illustrate the multiple and practical implications (or dilemmas) of word choice better than "The Beautiful American Word *Guy*," by John Weir:

> The beautiful American word "guy." It always gets me. For one thing, a guy is never alone. What if your name were Guy? Then you'd think that all the men behind all the deli counters on Ninth Avenue were talking to you. "What'll it be, Guy?" "Mayo, Guy?" "We're outta sesame, Guy, how about onion?" Guy is friendly, whereas "man" is hostile and competitive. "I hear you, man," actually means, "Back off, dickhead, I'm in charge here." "Dude" is useful, but thanks to Bart Simpson it's never sincere. "Buddy," "buster," and "pal" are sturdy but tainted by camp, like dialogue from old Hollywood movies. "Boss" scares me, and "chief" sounds undemocratic and maybe politically incorrect.
>
> I like "brother" sometimes. "Brother, you gotta be kidding," a truck driver yelled at me once on Eighth Avenue, because I was reading a book and crossing the street against the light. He twisted the word around to mean, "Die, motherfucker," but I'm a romantic, and I heard him saying, "Cling to me as we plunge together manfully into the abyss."
>
> Still, guy is the most inclusive and universally tender, taking the back of your neck in its creased palm and saying, "I'm counting on you." It's a promise and a threat, a stroke, a supplication, and a plea. If there were an epic poem of America in muscular four-beat Old English lines, its first word would not be "Hwaet," but "Guy."

Weir's poem rejoices in and agonizes over the wealth of alternative nouns by which one man can address another in American. Looked at as a dilemma of vocabulary, the poem can be seen as simply a catalog, or rehearsal, of available synonyms—each one with its own history, baggage, and connotations: *man, dickhead, chief, motherfucker, buddy.* Looked at as a predicament of masculinity, or politics, and we are deep inside not just the psyche but the history of the world.

To illustrate, consider one of the synonyms in Weir's poem, "chief." *Chief* has etymological roots in the word *chief* in Old French, and the word *capum* or *caput* in Latin, meaning *head.* But in the history of its usage, English users know the word from its frequent use in John Wayne movies, and from the popular-culture tales of cowboys and Indians; we involuntarily are reminded of stone-faced Native Americans, dressed in feathered headdresses. Likewise, we are aware of the latter-day controversy surrounding the use of *chief* as a label for this "American ethnic minority," a context to which the poem refers as "maybe politically incorrect." The circumstances of the word *chief,* like many words, are so complicated and enmeshed, they can't be easily shaken off.

Thus, to use any interesting word is not just to pinpoint one meaning but also to invoke a whole resonating web of vocabularies, contexts, and ideas. In this particular way, diction is very much an instrument of associative imagination, and one of the many modes of intellect that collaborate in the making of a poem.

Diction as a Focusing Device

Diction's greatest power lies in its conceptual precision—in its compressed embodiment of discriminating intelligence. If a speaker says, "I am a *connoisseur* of *hotdogs,*" we recognize that the description is a deliberately incongruous combination of high-class and low-class elements, of French nomenclature and American vernacular. The effect is comic, satirical, and conceptually precise; we intuit that the speaker, by applying one diction to the topic of another, is mocking certain kinds of pretension. Or perhaps he is affectionately acknowledging his own lack of sophistication. The layered implications are socially complex and intellectually compressed.

Diction in this sense can be most usefully thought of as a *focusing* system, one that operates on both conceptual and emotive levels. After all, diction is the main instrument of constructing *tone,* and it is tone that orients our attention and inflects our attitude toward a scene, a person, or a topic.

"Connoisseur of hotdogs" is a rather *garish* performance of mixed diction. Diction used in a more tempered, orchestrated way can be found in August Kleinzahler's poem "Watching Dogwood Blossoms Fall in a Parking Lot Off Route 46." The diction of the title itself—its juxtaposition of "Route 46" and "Watching Dogwood Blossoms"— brings into focus the poem's central theme: the coexistence of pastoral beauty and man-made reality. Here is most of the poem:

> Dogwood blossoms drift down at evening
>   as semis pound past Phoenix Seafood
>
> and the Savarin plant, west to the Turnpike,
>   Patterson or hills beyond.
>
> The adulterated, pearly light and bleak perfume
>   of benzene and exhaust
>
> make this solitary tree and the last of its bloom
>   as stirring somehow . . .
>
> as that shower of peach blossoms Tu Fu watched
>   fall on the riverbank
>
> from the shadows of the Jade Pavilion.

"Watching Dogwood Blossoms" is a kind of elegant still life, combining images of the modern and the bucolic. But the effectiveness of the poem is not merely a matter of contrasting juxtaposed nouns, such as *semis* and *peach blossoms*—nor is its intention merely ironic, although one feels the presence of that possibility. The poetical formality of phrases like "the last of its bloom" indicates that the speaker's claims for beauty are sincere. Even conventionally disagreeable phenomena are descriptively elevated to aesthetic status by diction choices. Pollution creates an "adulterated, pearly light," a phrase in which the Latinate formality of *adulterate* actually dignifies the contamination to which it refers. Likewise, *bleak* is a word choice of erudite expressiveness; *perfume* dresses up *benzene* and *exhaust*. Kleinzahler's pastoral poem registers a contest between the ugly modern and the beautiful eternal, but spiritual elevation is ultimately given the advantage by the relative weights of diction.

Through its lyrical, light-handed layering of mixed dictions toward a very particular conceptual focus, "Watching Dogwood Blossoms" makes a transcendental claim for beauty, achieved against the resistance of its own unpoetic landscape. By presenting simultaneously rapturous and realist perspectives, the diction of the poem actually *trains* our cognition, instructing us in how to perceive the world in a very particular way: skeptically, yet also receptively, and appreciatively.

Hayden Carruth's poem "Une Présence Absolue" is essentially a prayer, one that employs diction in a building pattern of gradual escalation and then, abrupt descent, moving from an increasingly sacred rhetoric to vulgar self-acknowledgment. The theatrical effect is to present and then to collapse the distance between two realities, through two dictions, in order to make a sharply focused composite:

> Not aware of it much of the time, but of course we are
> Heedless folk, under the distracting stars, among the great cedars,
> And so we give to ourselves casual pardon. It is there, though,
>   always,
> The continuum of what really is, what only is.
> The rest is babble and furiosity. Imagination, let me pay more
>   attention to you,
> You alone have this letting power; give me your own gift, which
>   is the one

absolution.

I am this poor stupid bastard half-asleep under this bridge.

The first half of Carruth's poem, though not radically elevated, contains a smattering of high-discourse formal inflections, in both vocabulary and syntax: "we are / Heedless folk . . . among the great cedars, / And so we give to ourselves casual pardon." *Heedless, pardon, babble, furiosity*—all these word choices invoke a formal literariness and the aura of serious public address. The poem reaches its rhetorical and emotional climax in lines five and six, at the speaker's reverent invocation of imagination.

What happens next, in the poem's abrupt final sentence—"I am this poor stupid bastard half-asleep . . ."—is a plunging demotion of the high diction that has immediately preceded it. In the speaker's blunt declaration of his own crudity and ignorance, we get an accurate, focused acknowledgment of the distance between heaven and earth, between human nature and divinity, between the speaker's aspiration and his own humble actuality. This satisfying dramatic effect carries a conceptual and emotional punch; a complex revelation wrought mostly through diction. Not only does Carruth's vocabulary de-escalate *(poor/stupid/bastard)*, but the meditation is suddenly grounded in a specific narrative moment and setting, "under this bridge." The speaker is no longer a talking meditative head, but a mere man, made of flesh in a lowly physical landscape.

Of course the modulations of diction are a continuum; throughout the poem, and in the course of a single sentence, word choices fluctuate in minute and nuanced ways. Even early in the poem, Carruth is toying with the equilibrium between lofty and plain rhetoric. The phrase "we are heedless folk," for example, gives off an aura of casual seriousness, because *heedless* is formal and almost archaic, whereas *folk* has a casual plainness to it. Similarly, *of course* is informal, while "among the great cedars" conveys an atmosphere of veneration, as does "we give to ourselves pardon." Had the poet wished to elevate his rhetorical register even more at this moment, he easily might have said, "we *grant* ourselves casual pardon." All such subtle, word-by-word choices are instrumental in the poet's careful orchestration of a building swell, which is then abruptly deflated by the last sentence of the poem. Carruth's poem is rhetorically expert, and diction is his primary tool.

The Material Imagination

The selective material imagination of a poem—that is, the poem's *nouns*—comprise a consequential diction of their own. To have a painting by Vermeer in a poem presents a worldview different from a poem containing a convenience store and a Ping-Pong table. To have a string quartet and a Port-A-Potty in the *same* poem suggests a democratic universe, and possibly an ironic or comically observant speaker. Some poems are more "mixed" than others.

Kleinzahler's poem "Watching Dogwood Blossoms," discussed earlier, can be lucidly understood solely on the basis of its nouns. On the one hand, declares the poem, "semis pound past"; on the other, "watching dogwood blossoms." On the one hand, the seafood market, and on the other, a memory of ancient Chinese poetry. The poet's appreciation of an impure world is precisely configured by the counterpoint of nouns in the poem.

Any poet who wishes to enlarge or revitalize her aesthetic range might simply introduce a more diverse vocabulary of *things* into her poetry. The love poet who can incorporate Tylenol and violin lessons into a sonnet to the beloved has dilated and complicated the poetics of romance.

Mixed Diction as Culture Fest

Varietal diction in a poem is also an expression of a culture's breadth, of the conversation that culture is having with itself, among its many parts. If language is equivalent to the consciousness of a nation or culture, the range of vocabulary used in any work of literature is to

some degree the representation of the range of cultural inclusiveness—
conscious and unconscious.

Such a view of mixed diction is *dialectical.* According to this vision
of poetry, mixed word choices, such as *concubine* and *pooch, precipitous*
and *bean counter, hula dance* and *Kervorkian,* mingle like citizens inside
a paragraph or stanza, shoulder each other aside and exchange gossip.
This potpourri of speech gives the reader an idea of the complex social
forces that must be accounted for in any description of reality.

To include, as Robert Pinsky does in his poem "Louie Louie," the
Beastie Boys (a white hip-hop band formed in the 1980s) and the
Scottsboro Boys (defendants in a 1931 racially motivated rape trial)
in the same poem makes a statement about the breadth, variety, and
contradictions of the known world:

> I have heard of Black Irish but I never
> Heard of White Catholic or White Jew.
> I have heard of "Is Poetry Popular?" but I
> Never heard of Lawrence Welk Drove
> Sid Caesar Off Television
>
> I have heard of Kwanzaa but I have
> Never heard of Bert Williams.
> I have never heard of Will
> Rogers or Roger Williams
> or Buck Rogers or Pearl Buck
> Or Frank Buck or Frank
> Merriwell At Yale.
>
> . . . .
>
> I have heard of the Pig Boy.
> I have never heard of the Beastie
> Boys or the Scottsboro Boys but I
> Have heard singing Boys, what
> They were called I forget.

I have never heard America
Singing but I have heard of I
Hear America Singing, I think
It must have been a book
We had in school, I forget.

Pinsky's poem may be a nonsense song, but it is also implicitly offered as a portrait of America. "Louie Louie" is a lyric about the complex dance of history, memory, artifact, and tribe. It suggests that we Americans are shallow but erudite, ignorant but sophisticated, and that we live suspended in an atmosphere of references of which we are mostly unconscious. The chant itself is a way of spraying an aerosol of names into the air, waking them up before stirring them back into the culture batter, in their broth of rhyme, memory, nonsense, and reason.

And the truth is, naming as a game is a primal oral pleasure that goes back to our childhood use of language—"Betty and Tiger sitting in a tree / K-I-S-S-I-N-G." "Mona got mono from Monroe in Morocco." Naming is a pleasure game that reminds us of learning the alphabet and skipping rope, and Pinsky's poem evokes that deep play activity with vocabulary for its own sake. Simply to move our mouths around the shifting shapes of our vocabulary is one of the deep levels of poetry pleasure.

Diction's Comic Possibilities

On these and other grounds, the intricate energies of diction offer great opportunity for comedy; the frictive sonic play between vowel and consonant, the endless combinatory possibilities for pace, the rhythmic play between single-syllable and polysyllabic words—it all constitutes a rich erotic field of amusement in itself. But diction's comedic power is also deeply social and cognitive. The comedy of diction almost always springs from the colliding energies of playfulness and utility. Words chosen and used for utility are usually pragmatically economical and semantically clear, what is called "transparent": "The dog slept in the shadow of the pickup truck." But word choices made for the sake of sonic pleasure, or for the sake of rhetorical inflation, or deflation, can easily exceed, ornament, distort, or derail the speech task purportedly at hand. "Jasper's geriatric bluetick lay comatose in the spilled shade of his Civil War–era Buick." Such riffing can be observed in the routines of any talented stand-up comedian—and almost any good comedic poet. *Lenny Bruce*

Sheer *excessiveness* of diction is a highly entertaining effect. Consider this hyperbolic and hyperactive passage from Barbara Hamby's verbose, comically alliterative "Betrothal in B minor," a treatise against marriage:

> . . . Oh, no, my dear
>
> mademoiselle, marriage is no *déjeuner sur l'herbe*,
> no bebop with Little Richard for eternity,
>
> no bedazzled buying spree at Bergdorf or Bendel,
> no clinch on the beach with Burt Lancaster.
>
> Although it is sometimes all these things, it is
> more often, to quote la Marquise de Merteuil, "War," . . .

Most good poetic users of diction, like Hamby, have great theatrical instincts, and are talented ventriloquists, or mimes, of speech mannerisms. The comedy of Hamby's tirade derives from her stylistic parody of a Victorian lecture, addled by the jazzed-up lexicon of the speaker's analogies—for instance, that marriage is "no bebop with Little Richard for eternity."

In Marianne Moore's "Critics and Connoisseurs," a largely straight-faced poem, we can see the way that a high affectedness of Latinate diction performs double functions: on the one hand, Moore exhibits a wonderful particularity, which seems intended and earned; on the other, Moore's polysyllabic, psychological, and abstract (Latinate) diction below, creates an ornamental, comically intellectualized affectedness—an impersonation of which the speaker is conscious. Truly, she has it both ways: theatrical *and* incisive:

> I remember a swan under the willows in Oxford,
>   with flamingo-colored, maple-
>   leaflike feet. It reconnoitered like a battle-
> ship. Disbelief and conscious fastidiousness were
>   ingredients in its
>   disinclination to move. Finally its hardihood was
>   not proof against its
>   proclivity to more fully appraise such bits
>   of food as the stream
>
>   bore counter to it; it made away with what I gave it
>   to eat.

Wallace Stevens is another example of a modernist poet who employs stylistically exaggerated diction, sometimes for gravitas, and sometimes for comedic clown-like purposes. His poem "Bantams in Pine Woods" begins with the sonically absurd, Dr. Seuss–like couplet:

> Chieftain Iffucan of Azcan in caftan
> Of tan with henna hackles, halt!

The pleasures here are sonic, comic, nutty, and childlike, crossing the line from sense making into joyful babble. Stevens, often represented to college students as the major philosopher of modern American poetry, is in fact one of its true comedians.

Mixed Diction as Heightened Mannerism

Some contemporary poems employ an especially heightened and hybrid vocabulary to create musical and textural effects that reach for atmospheres beyond the comical. Lucie Brock-Broido's evocative poetic language is often pitched far from the registers we know as conversational. The gorgeous, exotic lexicon of her poems is deliberately far-fetched; sometimes baroque enough to leave subject matter almost behind, as in "Basic Poem in a Basic Tongue":

Here is the maudlin petty bourgeoisie of ruin.

A sullen pity-craft before the fallows of Allhallowmas.

The aristocracy in one green cortège at the registry of Vehicle and Animus.

A muster of pale stars stationed like gazelles just looking-up,

Before the rustle of the coming kill.

At home, the hoi polloi keep tendering the books of Job's despond, in braille.

The girl at open half-door in her early Netherlandish light of melancholia.

So many brooding swans like floating inkstains on a lake of slender wakefulness.

Conventional questions about location, theme, and narrative will be somewhat frustrated here. What is the "maudlin petty bourgeoisie of ruin"? The musical texture of Brock-Broido's language is lush and beautiful, the sensibility aesthetically exaggerated, both in image ("A muster of pale stars stationed like gazelles") and in sound ("a sullen pity-craft before the fallows of Allhallowmas"). Brock-Broido's diction is self-consciously, exotically cranked up.

Nonetheless, in a manneristic, intentionally artificial mode like this, mixed diction is not to be held to strict semantic requirements;

the poem is more a demonstration of linguistic melodrama than it is a report from the realm of experience. One feels that the poetic language rejoices in its own flamboyance; it is an art of theatrical performance, with only a glance toward subject matter. Sound is as important to this aesthetic style as reference, even if reference is not left entirely behind. Moreover, the poem is still emotionally readable: a responsive reader will intuit the general atmosphere of narcotic, languorous mourning, and bathe in it.

Of the many craft elements to admire here, exotically mixed diction is surely one: *hoi polloi* and the books of Job, "the registry of Vehicle and Animus," and "the Netherlandish light of melancholia." Brock-Broido's coinages and combinations are sumptuous and decadent with a postmodern, sometimes tongue-in-cheek spin. In the defiantly titled "Basic Poem in a Basic Tongue," we are given a cornucopia of pure poetry, but we are not directed to any specific world beyond the poetic canvas. The allegiance to Beauty over Fidelity deploys the function of diction toward an aesthetic center of pleasure, not accuracy.

Although Brock-Broido's poem wanders freely beyond the known fields of sense, and even tinkers with inconsistency of tone, nonetheless the poem preserves a kind of commanding romantic intensity. Brock-Broido's poem is still—and the distinction is crucial—recognizably *expressive.* "Basic Poem in a Basic Tongue" intends to both seduce and mystify the reader with its sonic expressive romance.

The Aesthetic of Diction Disjointedness

As poetic diction moves further away from its tethered connectedness to things, further away from an identifiable context, we find poetry moving toward a realm of autonomous language constructions, something like abstract expressionist paintings. One can see the seed of such an impulse in Brock-Broido's poem. When we think about diction in experimental or postmodern poetry, we begin to encounter a host of unconventional agendas, motives, and practices: strategies flashy, dissonant, and sometimes cryptic. Such cutting loose of style from content has become a playground for experiment in American poetry.

This has consequences for poetry. When poetic vocabulary gets more and more unhinged from its specific conventional meanings, and becomes an end in itself, diction no longer is employed as a focusing device. This in itself is not a bad thing—the ravishments and nuancings of style are marvelous poetical constituents. But when diction is deliberately employed as a counterfeit currency, language may be rendered into a sort of art nouveau shell, hollow of meaning. Likewise, when diction is deployed to be intentionally dislocated and opaque, it can create an eccentric screen that is at once seductive and impenetrable. The venerable John Ashbery, our era's most prominent modernist, is a case in point. Ashbery's improvisations are very much composed of mixed dictions and idioms, and Ashbery has written many richly expressive poems—but he also has produced plenty of empty, arbitrary language structures, which exploit the motley character of American speech. Here is the first half of Ashbery's "Marivaudage":

> We are all patting sleeping shoes
> on a string. The board of selection
> takes precedence at such times as arise
> in the sky broken conduits and stresses
> and as such may be over, this time.
> Pass the Durkee's. And repent.
>
> Yes sir it shall be done unto you
> as the maze requests, fiber inspected
> and the president is eight months old.

Disjointedness is really the point of this stylistic exercise. "The board of selection takes precedence," "Pass the Durkee's," "it shall be done unto you." Ashbery's vocabulary of familiar speech samples is marvelously wide: it is a diction circus. Yet no single voice or tone dominates, and no context (pattern, theme, narrative, voice) is offered that might unify this diaspora. The extremely mixed discontinuity of "Marivaudage" reveals no focusing intention. Nor is the poem, on the other hand, like Brock-Broido's poem, working sonically to evoke a particular emotional atmosphere. Instead, Ashbery's anarchy is dissociative—his aesthetic intent is simply to make a kind of Lego lyric of odd parts. The import here is disarray, and the rich mix of diction is merely the buzz of sensation. To wrestle such a poem for significance is like pressing your ear to the side of a refrigerator and trying to guess its contents—what you hear is only electrical current moving through wires.

What's missing from "Marivaudage," and many other such "textual" experiments, are two related poetic values: emphasis and reciprocity. Without a discernible emphasis, without some hint of authorial allegiance assigned to some moment in the poem over others, we cannot begin the process of response. We need to be able to identify what and where the stakes are in a poem; where the gravity, or weight, is located. Ultimately, this amounts to *existential* commitment: knowledge or perspective that has been gained from suffering the world. Without such a stake or declaration, regardless of style, the poem will lack substance.

Similarly, without a reciprocal relationship between a poem and a reader, that is, a relationship that deepens through responsiveness and rereading, one of the most basic reasons for poetry has been inexplicably abandoned. At that point, virtuosity, verbal facility, and intelligence are beside the point. If the poem does not need the reader, the reader does not need the poem.

The Impossible Is Possible

Yet, in poetry almost anything is possible, and in fact, it *is* possible to employ radically exaggerated, manneristic, even disjunct, diction mixing in a powerfully successful poem. What is necessary for such aesthetic self-consciousness to be successful, however, is an anchoring intellectual or emotional occasion. This primary expressive motive must establish a reliable center of gravity in the poem's spectrum of diction. The second requirement follows from the first: the poem must build a relationship of trust and reciprocity with the reader, so that the poem rewards and responds to the reader's investment of attention.

Michael Palmer's "I Do Not" is an example of a poem that embraces artificiality and abrupt, multiple chord changes on the diction spectrum. Yet the poem guides and rewards the reader fully, by elliptically identifying the background occasion of the poem as a whole. In this case, the occasion is the subject of war, which accounts for the dyslexia of the speaker's displacements:

I do not know English.

I do not know English, and therefore I can have nothing to say
about this latest war, flowering through a nightscope in the
     evening sky.

I do not know English and therefore, when hungry, can do no
     more
than point repeatedly to my mouth.

Yet such a gesture might be taken to mean any number of things.

I do not know English and therefore cannot seek the requisite
permissions, as outlined in the recent protocol.

Such as: May I utter a term of endearment; may I now proceed
     to put
my arm or arms around you and apply gentle pressure;
may I now kiss you directly on the lips; now on the left tendon
of the neck; now on the nipple of each breast? And so on.

"I Do Not" presents a catalog of experiences that, contends the speaker, are unsayable—to him, at least. The shifts and strains between various dictions are evident. Yet what is also evident, from the very beginning of the poem, is the central background subject matter—war. That is the emphatic background, or context of the poem, in the foreground of which language itself is inadequate. Though the poem's journey drifts through diction cluster after diction cluster, our consciousness of the deep structure topic of war persists, and is in subtle ways reiterated:

> I do not know English. Therefore I have no way of communicating
> that I prefer this painting of nothing to that one of something.
> . . . .
> No way to differentiate the hall of mirrors from the meadow of
>   mullein, the beetlebung
> from the pinkletink, the kettlehole from the ventifact.
>
> Nor can I utter the words science, seance, silence, language and
>   languish.
>
> Nor can I tell of the arboreal shadows elongated and shifting
>   along the wall as the
> sun's angle approaches maximum hibernal declination.
> . . . .
> I cannot repeat the words of the Recording Angel or those of
>   the Angel of Erasure.
>
> Can speak neither of things abounding nor of things disappearing.
> . . . .
> Because I do not know English I have been variously called
>   Mr. Twisted,
>   The One Undone, the Nonrespondent, The Truly Lost Boy,
>   and Laughed-At-By-Horses.
>
> The war is declared ended, almost before it has begun.
>
> They have named it The Ultimate Combat between Nearness
>   and Distance.
>
> I do not know English.

Palmer's poem, on the one hand, announces the defeat of speech, but it does so in a poignant and sprawlingly inclusive way, anchored to an experiential occasion—war. Human activity continues, but the enterprise of war, and the profound dissonance of modern experience, negate the meaning of all other human activities and the speech for saying them. The result is a kind of dyslexia, or autism, which the speaker embodies. As in a play by Samuel Beckett, Palmer's negation of the sayable is resounding and provocative, moving and memorable, and shows some of the powerful capacity of modernist techniques.

"I Do Not" can be explored rewardingly at length, but merely to observe the motley array of dictions inside it suggests how a poem can manage to retain cohesion even while radically stretching those limits. Palmer successively visits and discards the dictions of intimacy, of appetite, of bureaucratic dissembling ("the requisite permissions, as outlined in the recent protocol"), of indigenous naming ("Laughed-At-By-Horses"), of prophecy. He plays chords of mannerist silliness ("No way to differentiate the hall of mirrors from the meadow of mullein, the beetlebung from the pinkletink, the kettlehole from the ventifact"), he slips and slides between the phonemic resemblances of *science* and *seance, language* and *languish.* The poem's deducible and very modernist inference is that none of this language suffices or manages to matter—and yet Palmer's linguistic brokenness is expressive, poignant, and reciprocates the reader's responsiveness.

American English is a great experiment in progress, and American poetry is its laboratory upon a hill. Several decades ago, the poet Tim Dlugos published a chapbook of poems with the title *Je Suis ein Americano,* as if making the point of this essay in brief. I suppose the mythic analogue might be the story of Frankenstein's monster. The creature we know as Frankenstein is patched together by a mad doctor, who employs a cut-and-paste method using the recycled parts of executed criminals. The monster escapes, descends from the mountain, and terrorizes the villagers. It sounds a lot like postmodernism, doesn't it? Yet the big, interestingly fabricated fellow is trying to communicate something—maybe he just wants a hug, but he can't make himself understood to the frightened townspeople. Their natural-enough tribal reaction is to try to kill him. In American poetry, too, the boundary between the natural and unnatural continues to shift, and American poets keep pushing the limits, searching for a creation at once wide awake and divine.

Idiom,
Our Funny Valentine

I am driving around Houston, listening to a sermon by one of our many local radio evangelists. Call him Pastor James. Brother James is telling an anecdote about himself. The end goes something like this:

> And in that moment, looking at that shiny outboard forty-four-horsepower engine, and my little nine-year-old daughter, I felt Jesus look into my heart, and I said, "I am *so* busted."

Big tender *oohs* and *ahhs* from the congregation; well deserved, too, wrought by the skill of a language man. In this case, it is the particular genius of idiom that evokes my admiration. "I am *so* busted," says the preacher, and the commonality between leader and flock is instantly evoked, renewed, and reestablished; the playing field leveled, the airwaves bathed in human warmth and intimacy. Time to pass the collection plate.

Most idiom has the contradictory status of seeming, on the one hand, like exhausted speech (i.e., it is used frequently and thoughtlessly), while at the same time it is very much alive with tribal flavor and the energy of the contemporary. Idiom shares categorical boundaries with vernacular, slang, colloquialism, and jargon. It pervades our speech, but what is it really, and how does it function—as it surely does—in the environment of a poem? The very fact that it is used in poems challenges the supposition that all poetic language must be fresh and particular. Nonetheless, much of idiom's sizzle comes not from its brand-new freshness but from its ripe familiarity.

In this instance, idiomatic phrase is also compounded and fused with slang—"busted" is vernacular for "arrested." But what is really remarkable about this verbal alchemy is its achieved transformation. Cunningly, the preacher recasts the elevated, somewhat scary concept of sin into something more domestic and negotiable, something on the level of getting a speeding ticket.

Idiom's great vitality is the quickness with which it fabricates intimacy between speaker and audience; in that way, it is a constituent element of voice, tone, and the creation of character. Likewise, idiom conveys complex connotative information. Most interestingly, perhaps, is the way idiom operates in the realm of half-consciousness. It flutters partly above and partly below the level of our attention. "You are so busted" has been baptized in so many mouths that the repetition has enhanced its power in one way, and dulled its edge in another. Thus, idiom is a symptom of language going to sleep, and also a device capable of waking it up.

One etymological meaning of idiom is "special property": *idios,* from the Greek, "one's own." It is *our* speech; how we talk; the way we say it here; we *own* it; we can do what we want with it. We are the people. Idiom is language that has a figurative meaning particular to the common use of a given speech culture. The dictionary says that there are twenty-five thousand idiomatic expressions in common American use. Our speech is rife with idiom; we use it in the way that animals deploy various smells and glands: to tell others who we are, and who we are with. Or, conversely, maybe we use it the way chameleons use color: to blend in.

A second characteristic of idiom that is intriguing, especially for poets, is the way idiom is often combinatory—a combination of words, a word group that has become, for all purposes, fused into a unit. When an idiomatic phrase is used as if it were a single word—"chunked" into a singular grammatical unit—it is what grammarians like John Saeed call *collocated,* or a *collocation:* "words that became affixed to each other until they have metamorphosed into a fossilized term." Such fused, compounded words develop a specialized meaning as an entity, as an idiom. "Houston, we have ignition" is an example.

You may hear an echo, embedded in the above definition of *collocation*, from Emerson's essay "The Poet." The archaeological image is Emerson's, coined in 1844, when archaeology was young:

> The etymologist finds the deadest word to have been once a brilliant picture. Language is fossil poetry. As the limestone of the continent consists of infinite masses of the shells of animalcules, so language is made up of images, or tropes, which now, in their secondary use, have long ceased to remind us of their poetic origin. But the poet names the thing because he sees it, or comes one step nearer to it than any other.

All language, says Emerson, originally arose from the ground of specific material experience. All language begins as metaphor. *You turn me on. At twenty-four she blossomed.* Emerson laments that we civilized folk live in the midst of our own linguistic wealth like people treading water at sea, people who hardly notice the water, ignorant of its vitality and vividness. When Emerson uses the term *fossilized*, his inflection is negative. It takes a Thoreau or a Whitman—a real poet, he says—to make the fossils come alive, to reconnect language to nature; to make dried blood wet again.

Idiom may indeed be a fossilized hunk of speech, fused together and forgetful of the occasion of its original inspiration, but even in this fossilized form, it has real power. For an example of idiomatic power in action, consider "Air Hostess," a poem by the great Israeli poet Yehuda Amichai, as translated from the Hebrew by Glenda Abramson:

> The air hostess said put out all smoking material,
> but she didn't specify, cigarette, cigar or pipe.
> I said to her in my heart: you have beautiful love material,
> and I didn't specify either.
>
> She told me to fasten and tie myself
> to the seat and I said:
> I want all the buckles in my life to be shaped like your mouth.

She said: Would you like coffee now or later
or never. And she passed me
tall as the sky.

The small scar high on her arm
showed that she would never have smallpox
and her eyes showed that she would never again fall in love:
she belonged to the conservative party
of those who have only one great love in their life.

"Air Hostess" is a poem of sexual drollery, hyperbole, and male sorrow. Although idiom is not *supposed* to be very portable between cultures, any contemporary traveler would feel an immediate pleasurable response to the idiomatic moments in Amichai's poem; the pleasure, for example, triggered by a phrase that has been collocated and fossilized from our collective cultural experience as fliers: "Put out all smoking materials." As of this writing, the No Smoking warning may be practically archaic, but it is still verbally alive.

Our first pleasure in reading this poem is one of *recognition*—not just of the narrative occasion but also of the rhetorical ceremony being invoked, the ritual speech of the airline experience. It is the whole collocated fossilized phrase that we hear: "Please fasten your seat belts." Our response is Pavlovian; it is like being tickled. Almost involuntarily we feel our status as expert users of cultural vocabulary; it a pleasure of memory and recurrence.

Secondarily, we delight in the poet's theft and adaptation of such phrase units to an alternative purpose: a story of desire and attraction, sexual wit and euphemism. "You have beautiful love material," says the speaker to himself, "and I didn't specify either." For all its casual effortlessness, it is a funny and complex operation: taking a scrap of culturespeak, exploiting its powers of semiconscious familiarity, and then fashioning a fresh metaphorical euphemism out of the diction: *and I didn't specify either.*

To track the shifting linguistic field of Amichai's poem is to notice that he uses idiom alternately with and in counterpoint to metaphor. "I want all the buckles in my life to be shaped like your mouth"; "You have beautiful love material." The talent Amichai is most famous for is metaphor, which is part of why he translates so well. But here we can see how good he is with tone, with irony, with syntactic pattern, and narrative. And with idiom.

In stanza three, Amichai returns to the strategy of his previous success, and draws from socially familiar, collocated language: "Would you like coffee now or later." Again, the speaker elicits the frisson of recognition—then, swiftly, deploys the poetic maneuver by which the familiar is modified, made new, and extended in an unexpected direction: "now or later / or never."

That word, *never*, with its little fatalistic chime, is the first dark note of the poem; *never*, which rhymes Eros with death, and marks the speaker as an aging mammal. *Would you like it, now, later . . . or never?* is what he hears; the options not just for coffee, but love, or life. Oh yes, now we remember—carpe diem! There are *nevers* in this world, lots of them. The first riff on conventional airplane speech was developed as a lewd comedy routine; but now the poem's tone dips into a more shadowy theme: the finiteness of life and the lapse of erotic possibility.

Amichai shifts back to his default setting, metaphor, to augment the suggestion: "And she passed me / tall as the sky." The image does what image is supposed to—it infers and reemphasizes the unattainability of what one might want, of what is *not* on the menu, and the speaker's disappointment.

"Air Hostess" concludes with a few quick turns of metaphorical genius, in a passage that combines the syntactical force of parallelism with the imagistic and conceptual power of analogy:

> The small scar high on her arm
> showed that she would never have smallpox,
> and her eyes showed that she would never again fall in love:
> She belonged to the conservative party
> of those who have only one great love in their life.

The richness and complexity of analogy here are wonderful. It might seem that the speaker is just narrating or describing, but work into the text and you'll notice the inferences borne by images: that desire is like smallpox, and the stewardess's reserved eyes are vaccination scars. Love is a disease, against which some people get defensively vaccinated. Amichai's metaphor further implies that the "conservative" style of love protects the individual from the ever-present danger and power of Eros. And, the speaker's tone suggests, this immunity is something of a tragedy.

Amichai's poem shows all the cunning and seductive power of idiom use, in addition to his other trademark skills. It's the balancing and orchestration of these various skills in concert that make him so masterful. He makes it look easy, but it *is* rocket science. As we leave the poem, the poet's love material have been put out, but they are still smoking.

Cheap Populism and the Loss of Standards

Certain writers are temperamentally drawn to the flavors and uses of idiom. These are poets who traffic with the temporal, the temporary, the current zeitgeists of culture and language. What names come to mind? E. E. Cummings, Anne Sexton, Carl Sandburg, Frank O'Hara, Robert Frost, Nikki Giovanni, Catullus, Constantine Cavafy, Amiri Baraka, Wisława Szymborska, Charles Bukowski, William Stafford, Diane Wakoski, Billy Collins. These are the poets who, in another world, would be on baseball cards; poets who, more and less, use a style that calculatedly draws on the glamour of familiarity. They are the ones who rejoice in the milieu of the contemporary, convinced that the local, the regional, and the transient have a poetic flavor and representational legitimacy equal to more elevated, denatured, universal language. They are that dreadful thing: *populists.*

Writers as various as Basho and Bahktin have said that a poem is "a personal language purified of the clichés of the tribe." Maybe such an assertion intends a distinction between the vernacular and the classical style; the classical mode, perhaps, aspires to language *cleansed* of region and era, language that can't be reduced to any particular place and time. The idiomatic poet, however, is committed to more demotic, dirty, culturally entangled speech.

Given the quick intimacy of idiom, it is easy to predict the potential for its abuse—of using it to get cheap laughs. Just think of a stand-up comic, saying "size matters" or "major food group," as in, "He thinks beer is a major food group." Or, "Step away from the vehicle, Tiffany." Stand-up comedians and sitcoms are admirable for their fluency in idiom, and sometimes shameless in squeezing every bit of freshness out of anything that works.

For the poet, or the reader, one relevant question arises: At what point does the use of idiom in art and poetry translate into dumbing things down for the sake of chummy appeal? What is the distinction, the line between idiom and cliché? Or between the cheap source of electricity represented by the natural resource of idiom, and the laziness of tired or manipulative speech? Between art and entertainment? Is the use of idiom as a kind of linguistic comfort food essentially a bad habit for a poet to fall into?

These are real questions, ones that I can imagine a lonely spoken-word poet asking himself late at night, while looking at an application to an MFA program. The counterversion of this insecurity is to imagine how Richard Wilbur would feel at a Billy Collins concert.

Of course, the greatest danger for the idiomatic poet, the voice poet, the easy-listening poet is lowballing the poem in ambition or concept. Idiomatic can mean automatic. Populist can mean people-pleasing.

At the same time, most poems *are* composed of repetitive motions. It's not just apprenticeship that is imitative but our whole careers. The same poems get written over and over. *My cat died and I'm sad. Why don't you love me more accurately? Those leaves are nice. Janice and Harvey's marriage was full of sandpaper. God moved to Las Vegas and left no forwarding address.* In fact, these poems need to be written and rewritten in the idiom and the tenor of the age. Their testimony needs to be renewed, their currency to be sustained.

To acknowledge the redundancy of art should not encourage any writer to be lazy, or to coast. It takes a lot of work and talent and even courage to *rewrite* the great poems and stories of the past. Very infrequently does a work of art break the crust of our collective and respective sleep, crack the plaster cast of its conventions, burst up fresh from the coffin, the husk of the self, the crypt of the tradition, and shriek the cry of the peacock. Randall Jarrell said that even a very good poet is one who, in a lifetime of standing out in thunderstorms, manages to get hit once or twice by the lightning of great art. And before we overromanticize some notion of absolute originality, remember that when a "classic" poem or song *is* written, it seems at once brand new and as if it already existed. Brand new, it sounds utterly familiar.

Meanwhile, idiom has its own strong poetic tradition, of poems that are *not* striving to break the mold. Like Catullus, as translated by Charles Martin, in his poem 112:

> You're just too much, Naso—too much for most men to handle,
> although you're certainly willing to handle most men.

Catullus, that crowd-pleasing satyr, satirist, and demotic poet, constructs his poem from a play on familiar figurative speech, which operates by raising the meaning of a phrase out of its idiomatic rut, and back into its literal, mechanical meaning. He counterpoints the idiom of "to handle" (too much to manage) with "to handle" (fondle). That Naso is just *too much*. Such sleight of hand may look easy, but one should note that, two thousand years after composition, the poem is still in print.

So, is idiom the low road? Or does it deserve more respect than it gets?

The Unconsciousness of Idiom

That question brings us to a poem by Lawrence Ferlinghetti, a poet who, in a more poetically democratic America, would have been poet laureate some decades ago. Here is his poem "Sometime During Eternity":

Sometime during eternity
some guys show up
and one of them
who shows up real late
is a kind of carpenter
from some square-type place
like Galilee
and he starts wailing
and claiming he is hip
to who made heaven
and earth
and that the cat
who really laid it on us
is his Dad
. . . . . .
You're hot
they tell him

And they cool him

They stretch him on the Tree to cool
And everybody after that
is always making models
of this Tree
with Him hung up
and always crooning His name
and calling Him to come down
and sit in
on their combo
as if he is <u>the</u> king cat
who's got to blow
or they can't quite make it

Only he don't come down
from His Tree

Him just hang there
on His Tree
looking real Petered out
and real cool
and also
according to a roundup
of late world news
from the usual unreliable sources
.real dead

If we look down on this poem from our high brows, do we not fault our own pleasure? This poem, written in the 1950s, is companionably rich with idiom ("show up," "laid it on us," "you're hot"), and its compelling warmth is still alive.

"Sometime During Eternity" belongs to a tradition—not merely that of the Beat but also the one in which old stories are reinvigorated by a local teller—the way in which our familial ties are evoked through common knowledge of the tribal slang. Ferlinghetti's poem translates Western civ into hipster diction. Beatnik idiom tells gospel story. Both story and idiom are refreshed by the conjunction. The intimacy of the idiom warms us with recognition.

"Sometime During Eternity" is both a humorous and a serious poem, for the hipster speaker is, we recognize from his idiom, no stranger to spiritual aspiration. He has a religion of jazz combos and finger snapping, of cool cats who lay it on you. Yet he also is conversant with skepticism, and a wry sadness about the failed project of transcendence, and the deformities and self-deceptions of mainstream Christianity. The tension between the speaker's low vernacular and the high-traditional nature of the story embodies the mixed feelings of the poem—passionate sincerity, deep disappointment, protective irony. In Ferlinghetti's jargon, we feel the confident coherence and vectored coordination of speaker, audience, story, vocabulary, rhythm, and idiom.

Many literary critics now label Ferlinghetti a "minor Beat poet"; he's getting dropped from the anthologies for his cheap populism, for his perfection of the populist poetic hook. Yet one still meets under-graduates who, at some library sale in Ohio, stumbled upon *A Coney Island of the Mind* (published in 1956) and were illuminated by what poetry turned out to be. Ask yourself what poet first set the hook of poetry in you: if it was Bukowski or Cummings, or Ferlinghetti or Ginsberg or Anne Sexton, or Carl Sandburg—all populist, idiomatic poets. Then reconsider your condescensions.

Given all the affirmative things I feel justified in saying about Ferlinghetti's poem, I wonder at my own uneasiness in presenting it as an example of first-rate art. Is it because I am a little embarrassed about my own populist allegiance? In a conversation with a fiction-writing friend, the answer came to me: the poem has too much clo-sure. "Sometime During Eternity" is almost perfectly executed, but the door at the end of the poem doesn't open into possibility or un-certainty. As is often the case with poetic closure, the poem's end is too sure of itself, even smug. The door is slammed. Christ really *is* dead in the end of Ferlinghetti's poem, and that becomes its main point. Neither longing nor mystery is allowed to survive that thirst for clo-sure. That is the real end, man.

Another way to put this is that Ferlinghetti's poem is perhaps too direct, too frontal. Refer to the Amichai poem, whose stakes are apparently smaller, and ask yourself why it feels like a better poem. The answer is that "Air Hostess" is more nuanced and indirect. The apparent conclusion of that poem is not, in fact, the real conclu-sion. The speaker's apparent sympathy (and lust) for the stewardess is a facade and barricade for his own sense of loss and anticipation of death. The speaker's own vulnerable inner life, loneliness, and sorrow are actually the true and precisely constructed core of the poem. In this way, Amichai's poem may be smaller in scale but is larger, deeper, more empathetic, and more resonant than "Sometime During Eternity."

Idiom and the idiomatic mode are not to be held responsible for Ferlinghetti's slight lowballing in this instance. One might hypothe-size, however, that the poet's perfection of the idiomatic groove, at that time in his career, may also have made him a little lazy.

Big Hooks and Little Hooks

Songwriters are familiar with the concept of a hook, and so are poets. The hook concept is relevant in discussing the poetic use of idiom. A good idiomatic phrase in a poem can lift off at a crucial moment, striking the chord of tribal lingo at the same moment the poem is engaging some other business. It is no accident that the idiomatic poet is susceptible to composing for the music of the demotic phrase.

The idiomatic poet thinks and hears in phrase units. When you broaden the criteria for what constitutes idiom, to include phrase units that are more or less fused together by our habits of usage, it begins to seem like idiom constitutes a whole floating submerged structural system, of units collocated by habits of usage, a prosody that holds our language tribe together like the glue in the binding of a book.

Also, it turns out that there are such things as loud and soft hooks, big hooks and little hooks; our common speech is rife with them. Even such a minor and innocuous-seeming, almost bland phrase as "do not care" is collocated: "Mrs. Peabody does not care to say where she was at noon on the twenty-seventh." *Somewhere over the rainbow. Don't move a muscle. Hold that thought. I can't get over you.* "It's a figure of speech," in fact, is a figure of speech. We hear these units almost without hearing them; we deploy idiom without consciously choosing to; *it* guides us. The big insight in our era of poetics is that we live *inside* language, and that insight has affected American poetic practice profoundly.

Heather McHugh's Song of Idiom

Heather McHugh's poem "I Knew I'd Sing" capitalizes on and digs deep into the black dirt of American tribal speech bites. McHugh's poem acknowledges that one's cultural speech is a kind of hypnotic razzle-dazzle, a medium that incarcerates us as much as enables us. This tribal language can be oppressive; it has to be seized, hijacked, and repossessed to be made legitimate again.

Thus McHugh's poem begins with a catalog of idioms for behav-

ior, and ends with a proclamation that also rides the rhythm of fossilized speech:

> A few sashay, a few finagle,
> Some make whoopee, some
> make good. But most make
> diddly-squat. I tell you this
>
> is what I love about
> America—the words it puts
> in my mouth, the mouth where once
> my mother rubbed
>
> a word away with soap. The word
> was *cunt*. She stuck that bar
> of family-size in there
> until there was no hole to speak of, so
>
> she hoped. But still
> I'm full of it—the cunt,
> the prick, short u, short i,
> the words that stood
>
> for her and him. I loved
> the thing they must have done,
> the love they must have made, to make
> an example of me. After my lunch of Ivory I said
>
> *vagina* for a day or two, but knew
> from that day forth which word struck home
> the more like sex itself.
> I knew when I was big I'd sing
>
> a song in praise of cunt—I'd want
> to keep my word, the one with teeth in it.

> Even after I was raised, I swore
> nothing but nothing would be beneath me.

"I Knew I'd Sing" shows the rich utility of idiom, but not in a warm and fuzzy way. McHugh's poem strains to wake up words whose edges and origins have been forgotten. Here the speaker "stands by" words. "I'm full of it," she says, and means full of tribal speech. Her style veers between a kind of stoned scat singing and a hyperacuity about meanings. In that sense, the speaker of the poem exemplifies both the narcotic quality and the alertness of idiom.

In "I Knew I'd Sing," language is at once a habit, a dream, and a socially complicit instrument in our lives—an instrument we use, and will be used by. McHugh's ear is deeply idiomatic, and seems to hear all phrases overlaid and murmuring at once. The path she picks through this babble rubble is both attached to the background of usage patterns, and also willfully intent on its own zigzag but urgent journey of psychic necessity.

"This is what I love about / America," says the speaker—a phrase that should, after all the jingoistic occasions on which it has been spoken, instill into our hearts a dread of what comes next. But whereas a clichéd usage "empties" the meaning out of the idiom, McHugh hijacks the familiar, turning it into power for the individual. To cite an idiom that President Obama has used in one of his speeches, she knows how to hit a straight lick with a crooked stick. "This is what I love about / America—the words it puts / in my mouth." Brave and omnivorous, the speaker eats the soap, and the dirt the soap covers. The poet dives into the dumpster of idiom, marches into the poppy fields of our speech, yet is not anesthetized to sleep. "I loved / the thing they must have done," she says, "to make / an example of me."

Making It New

This issue of the tiredness, the threadbareness, the amnesiac erosion of habit and the rebuilding of language is fascinating. Emerson, remember, lamented that our daily speech is like the crumbling ruin of a once great civilization: and it's easy to agree with him today, when contemporary language is so flooded and degraded, so increased in volume and decreased in richness.

The bad news is true: we are always losing valuable parts of language, witnesses to dying and withering grammatical distinctions; daily we encounter instances of our declining collective facility with complex sentences.

But we should remember, too, that language is infinitely elastic and self-renewing; subject not only to dimmings and obsolescence but also to additions, reconstruction, and reinvigoration: *friend me; unfriend me; top kill; junk shot.* It's like a vast coral reef, an enormous organism, parts of it conscious, parts unconscious, parts dying and parts rising into audibility. In this ecosystem of American English, the archaic coexists with the brand new; the conventions shift backward, forward, and sideways and at different velocities, and for different reasons.

And Emerson, who brings the bad news, characteristically also has something hopeful to say about the regenerative capacities of language and consciousness:

> Genius is the activity which repairs the decay of things, whether wholly or partly of a material and finite kind. Nature, through all her kingdoms, insures herself. Nobody cares for planting the poor fungus: so she shakes down from the gills of one agaric countless spores, any one of which, being preserved, transmits new billions of spores to-morrow or next day.

The closer one looks, the clearer it becomes that categories of language are constantly fused, buried inside and echoed by each other. We discover that poetic speech is always changing in subtle registers, and that, as it runs its scales of tone and shade, it dips toward and away from vernacular and formality. As it summons up various etymologies, it also summons up whole slabs and slices of codified slang, phrase-length or sometimes speech-length compoundings and alloys of referent.

The use of idiom, and perhaps all poetry, is engaged in this constant, changing tension between familiar and unfamiliar, the power of old and the power of new, between idiom and experience, between the invention of new phrases, and the utilization of well-worn conventions.

With every poem and page a poet is choosing a relation to the language we have used, are using, and may use in the future. We inherited the page in a dream, and we will, mostly, write words that have been written before, in the same sequences, echoing the poems that we have read and heard. That is not, in fact, insignificant work. For better or worse, the responsibility is upon us. We are maintaining, renovating, and maybe sometimes adding to the size of the world we live and speak in. It's ours.

Litany, Game, and Representation: Charting the Course from the Old to the New Poetry

In his *Ninth Duino Elegy,* Rilke hypothesizes that the cosmic purpose of human beings on earth, surprisingly enough, might not be procreation, or penance, but *speech:*

> Are we, perhaps, here just for saying: House,
> Bridge, Fountain, Gate, Jug, Olive tree, Window,—
> possibly: Pillar, Tower? . . . . but for saying, remember,
> oh, for such saying as never the things themselves
> hoped so intensely to be.

Rilke outlines a sweet employment situation for poets: a kind of stewardship of creation. The poet names, and his speech vivifies material reality *(Olive tree, Window)* by pronouncing it. To name, according to Rilke, is to recognize and endorse the external world, to *encourage* it; and, through that encouragement, to illuminate and spiritualize it.

Rilke's theology recasts a story we already know: Adam's task of assigning the first names. As in that story, Rilke's scenario suggests a sacred relationship between three elements: the poet, the word, and the thing. The human is redeemed by the unique usefulness of his speech; language *increases* reality; matter is elevated by recognition. Rilke implies that the cosmic breach between spirit and matter can be healed when we address, through the act of naming, the world of creation.

Though Rilke finished his *Elegies* in 1923, very much inside the twentieth century, he seems remarkably untouched by what is called the modernist sensibility. In his mission of numinous pronouncement, he is untroubled by the possibility of any misfit between words and things; he has no fear of inaccuracy or misrepresentation. He doesn't worry about the shortcomings of language, or the arbitrariness of words, or the unknowability of everything. For him, speech seems to be a marvelous and natural, or even better, *supernatural,* act. As a poet, he feels adequate to his cosmic and profoundly simple mission.

Such confidence about the harmony between speech, things, and humans has not been universally shared in the twentieth century (it was not even shared by Rilke's more modernist contemporaries). Our faith in the adequacy of language has substantially eroded in the past hundred years, as has our belief in "knowledge," perception, and the integrity of human nature.

All these and many other kinds of insecurity have sorely challenged modern poets, as well as priests and scientists. After all, the poet who cannot confidently trust that the words *olive* and *tree* mean *a tree that makes olives* is working with a serious handicap.

This is a literary challenge, but also a profoundly human one. The crevasse between speech and matter is nothing less than a metaphysical wound to the human soul. It is identical with the split between human nature and nature itself—the wider the gap, the greater our very real sense of not belonging to the world. If language itself is a broken bridge, humanity is caught in a permanent condition of exile and alienation.

Even so, poetry has been resourceful; modern and contemporary poets have improvised a rich repertoire of aesthetic responses to the uncertainty of modern naming. It might be said, in fact, that to comprehend the manners and strategies of contemporary poetry, one has to recognize these strategies as responses to the dilemma of broken naming. The literary genre of the litany—a form that names and catalogs—offers a convenient showcase of individual poems through which to consider some of the approaches poets are taking to what has become the "problem" of naming the world.

"Are we, perhaps, here just for saying: House, / Bridge, Fountain . . . ?," asks the Rilkean poet. The urge is close to the roots of speech and poetry; the itemized praise for the parts of the world. That desire, to glorify by naming, must have been what animated the British poet Christopher Smart, in roughly 1760, when he made his ode to a housecat:

> For I will consider my Cat Jeoffry.
> For he is the servant of the Living God, duly and daily serving him.
> For at the first glance of the glory of God in the East he worships in his way.
> For is this done by wreathing his body seven times round with elegant quickness.
> For then he leaps up to catch the musk, which is the blessing of God upon his prayer.
> For he rolls upon prank to work it in.
> For having done duty and received blessing he begins to consider himself.
> For this he performs in ten degrees.
> For first he looks upon his forepaws to see if they are clean.
> For secondly he kicks up behind to clear away there.
> For thirdly he works it upon stretch with the forepaws extended.
> For fourthly he sharpens his paws by wood.
> For fifthly he washes himself.
> For sixthly he rolls upon wash.
> For seventhly he fleas himself, that he may not be interrupted upon the beat.
> For eighthly he rubs himself against a post.
>
> (*Jubilate Agno,* Fragment B, lines 695–710)

Smart's sleek, joyful litany embodies some primary premises about poetic speech: In the meticulousness of his observation, he reveals his faith in the *ability* of language to precisely convey. Likewise, we can deduce that he believes in the *obligation* of the psalmist to be accurate in his depictions. Third, the poet of *Jubilate Agno* feels entitled to exercise his own *inventiveness,* licensed to add verbal and imaginative flourishes, which, in this context, mimic the gusto of the cat itself ("For then he leaps up to catch the musk"). As postmodern, more

self-conscious writers than Smart, we may well envy his freedom from
linguistic doubt, his confidence that words are enough; that the world
does not revolt against being named; that words do not betray material reality. The result is an athletic song of praise with both naturalness
and literary flourish.

Illuminating, then, to scroll forward through the pages of literary
time, and consider the contemporary poem "Wildflower," by Stanley
Plumly. Like the Smart poem, "Wildflower" is a poem of loving praise,
a poem of naming, and a poem in contact with the sensory universe
of nature. But it is also a poem into which linguistic insecurity has en-
tered: a poem that has been forced to make the flawed, slippery aspect
of naming part of its subject matter, part of its approach to "truth":

> It is June, wildflowers on the table.
> They are fresh an hour ago, like sliced lemons,
> with the whole day ahead of them.
> They could be common mayflower lilies of the valley,
>
> daylilies, or the clustering Canada, large, gold,
> long-stemmed as pasture roses, belled out over the vase—
> or maybe Solomon's seal, the petals
> ranged in small toy pairs
>
> or starry, tipped at the head like weeds.
> They could be anonymous as weeds.
> They are, in fact, the several names of the same thing,
> lilies of the field, butter-and-eggs,
>
> toadflax almost, the way the whites and yellows juxtapose,
> and have "the look of flowers that are looked at,"
> rooted as they are in water, glass and air.
> I remember the summer I picked everything,
>
> flower and wildflower, singled them out in jars
> with a name attached.

Plumly's speaker wishes to name and to praise, but grows uneasy about this activity. He would *like* to praise the flowers as confidently and generously as Smart does his cat, but things are more complicated than that. The flowers have more than one name—which is the right one? Not only that, but the speaker's memory is unreliable. There was a day when the speaker knew the singular names of things, and trusted them—when everything had "a name attached." But now the bridge of language has broken, and a gulf has opened between himself and the physical world.

This loss of language is also a lamentation for lost youth, which is synonymous with lost certainty. The older, less trusting, and less trustworthy speaker names the flowers now as if stabbing at something he can't get exactly right. "They could be X," he says. "They could be Y." Thus the poem tells the tale of a fall from grace—not just from youth into the uncertainty of adulthood but also into alienation. He is disconnected from the creation. The estrangement from the natural world and the estrangement from language have become symptomatic of each other.

It seems appropriate that the speaker, midpoem, cites T. S. Eliot's wry, cross-eyed description of flowers: the flowers have "the look of flowers that are looked at." In this post-natural existence, in which man has slipped into the maze of self-consciousness, all things recede into the distant mirror. It is impossible to get any closer to X than the sign for X.

Plumly's speaker-poet has a case of language cross-eyes, a modern bifocal condition that has only worsened for poets over the past thirty years. This double vision, as we shall see, can lead to a host of speech impediments like stuttering, dyslexia, and muteness. The next generation of poets would contract a case of dislocation influenza that makes Plumly's linguistic uneasiness look like the sniffles.

Some Background Perspective

Linguistic insecurity! It has been with us long enough that we have developed, ironically, a rich technical vocabulary with which to describe

it. We have never mistrusted language more than in our postmodern
era. As the first line of a John Ashbery poem declares, "You can't say it
like that anymore." We have a general sense of the shiftiness and inaccuracy of words, of what the critic Marjorie Perloff calls the *indeter-
minacy* of language; and we feel the impermanence and imperfection
of any kind of knowing.

In addition to whatever existential causes there might be for this
condition, media and consumer culture have added heavily to the erosion and corruption of our faith in language. Most of the language we
encounter in daily life attempts some sort of manipulation, or con-
ceals some motive. Disillusioned by politicians and consumerism, our
acute mistrust of public speech is a sensible response. Naturally, this
mistrust has had an impact on poetic practice. It has destroyed an in-
nocence we once had about the word—which has resulted, in turn, in a
poetics of self-conscious style, irony, and circumlocution.

To get a taste of the way in which the subject of language itself
moves ever more prominently into the foreground of poetic practice,
compare the contemporary poem "Guidance Counseling," by Dean
Young, to the poems by Smart and Plumly. Young's poem, which similarly includes a catalog of names, playfully adopts the premise of being
a kind of *Kama Sutra*, a sex manual:

> When the woman, her shoulders on the bed,
> lifts her pelvis into the standing man,
> it is called Dentist Office. When the man,
> after an hour hiding in the closet, couples
> with she of the silk flowered dress, snug
> in the bodice, it is called Representational
> Democracy. When the woman licks her burnt
> finger, Tiny Garden Hose. Often as we grow
> old, life becomes a page obscured with
> too many words, like the sea with too many
> flashes. Like my screaming may obscure
> my love for you. How will we ever understand

each other? When the woman sits on the ladder
and the man churns like a lizard, stiff
in melting ice cream, it is called Many Dews.

"Guidance Counseling" does not suffer from the sorrowful tone
of existential unease we find in Plumly's poem, but here too language
is a problem: "How will we ever understand / each other?" Young's
poem is not obviously about the failure of speech, but tells a tale of
comical disjointedness. Language is seen as a kind of slippery im-
pediment between people. Poetic attention has been shifted from the
realm of *nature* (perception) to the realm of *language,* naming. The
poem could be said to be celebratory, even erotic, in its playfulness—
but it also emphasizes the disturbing, nutty arbitrariness of the act of
naming: Tiny Garden Hose; Representational Democracy; Dentist
Office. If we listen closely, we can recognize that these comical coinages are in fact a parody, an echo, of commercial brand names, such
as might be used to name perfumes, sell ice cream flavors, or catalog
paint chips.

Young's poem celebrates the cornucopia of phenomena. It playfully suggests that there is a rich universe of experience to be encountered. But the difference between Young's poem and what Christopher
Smart or Rilke were up to is substantial. Our wonder has acquired a
wry self-consciousness, and is directed not toward nature but toward
the radical elasticity of language, and the stylistic dexterity of artifice.

The Disconnect Goes Further

The disconnect between words and things can grow still more extreme
in contemporary poetic practice, as can the emphasis on language as
the preeminent subject matter of poetry. For example, consider the
following poem by a New York poet, Jordan Davis. "Woman (A.S.)"
is a declarative litany, but what is being litanized? Is there any actual
event or experience behind the poem? Or is it the "fiction" of naming
that is being demolished?

The red moon is a banjo
A jinx is a flat rate
I am a dropshot
Arizona is the sunrise of a fuckoff
Tonight is the uncompiled code of an iced coffee
A dart is the jimmy of a limousine
My homeland is the dogma of brimming
Turpentine is the Paul McCartney of your letting me know
My lever is tomorrow
A starling is a skinny boy
A drifter is a paragraph
Dehydration was your joyride
Pacman is a percentage
Spelling is diamonds
The grey grass is conformist
Her hat is Alaska . . .

Davis's poem is one more representation of the shift in the poet's relationship to the word, and of a radical loss of faith in the veracity of naming. "A Woman (A.S.)" seems pointedly intent on "neutralizing" some of our most deeply held assumptions about poetic language—that words are signs for "pointing," for instance; that a poem is "about" something; that metaphor serves a function of equation; even of the assumption that a poem is a message passing between two people. Nor does Davis's poem "accumulate" in any conventional way; it does not, as it progresses, acquire more meaning, or emotional significance, or more coherence. In this particular poem, all these conventional presumptions about a poem are discarded and replaced by a flamboyant style, which also serves as a lesson about postmodern language.

A conservative response to such a poetic mode might be to dismiss "Woman (A.S.)" as shallow; to ascribe to Davis a poetic nihilism, or terminal irony. Yet the evidence does not really support such a reading. Davis's poem exhibits too much youthful pleasure and gusto to be written off as cynically hip or merely disillusioned. It is as if, freed by a disaffection with conventional language use, the fields of play are open to indefinable adventure. Anything equals anything! In our postmodern era of deeply mistrusted speech, it is a paradoxical fact that this uninhibited sense of play is common in some of the new poetry. The alienation, angst, and unease of one generation—Plumly's, for example—becomes the liberating poetic license of the next. The childlike pleasure of Davis's speaker in inventing language is evident, as are the evocation and subversion of grammatical structures. It is all turned into play, and we would be mistaken to dismiss play itself as shallow. Even if the modern chasm between words and things has grown so large as to make naming absurd, poetry can still make language into a kind of pure dance.

Still. For all its spirit of play, Davis's poetry is a symptom of the "dislocation" of word from thing for many contemporary American poets. Davis's poem is also unmistakably ironic, with its specialized tongue planted deep in its linguistic cheek. Here, a language "system" takes aesthetic center stage, displacing the poetry of experience.

Another Piece of Perspective

Much new poetry, in contrast to the poetry of thirty and forty years ago, is, like Davis's poem, deeply engaged in technique. Preoccupied with formal experiment and matters of style, it celebrates its own artifice. It is not so obsessed with "capturing" anything, or psychological struggle, or apprehending a "truth." Instead, it is involved in exploring representation as an end in itself. The critic Stephen Burt claims that "epistemology and theories of language—how we know what we know, how we say it—have become as central to contemporary lyric as psychoanalysis in the late 1950s, myth and politics in the late '60s." The New Poetry, says Burt, is not "about" politics or psychology, but about how we perceive, and how language affects that perception. Thus, the physics of representation often holds the foreground of many poems now.

A contemporary poem that elegantly and wittily embodies the preoccupation of the New Poetry with language, and its emphasis on perspective, is the second section of Robert Hass's long, ambitious poem "My Mother's Nipples." It, too, is a litany, but its preoccupying subject is *how* things are said, not *what* is said:

> *The cosmopolitan's song on this subject:*
>
> Alors! les nipples de ma mère!
>
> *The romantic's song*
>
> What could be more fair
> than les nipples de ma mère?
>
> *The utopian's song*
>
> I will freely share
> les nipples de ma mère.
>
> *The philosopher's song*
>
> Here was always there
> with les nipples de ma mère
>
> *The capitalist's song*
>
> Fifty cents a share
>
> *The saint's song*
>
> Lift your eyes in prayer
>
> *The misanthrope's song*

I can scarcely bear

The melancholic's song

They were never there,
les nipples de ma mère.
They are not anywhere.

Here, in the middle of an autobiographical meditative poem about family and loss, is a litany of adroit examples of how different kinds of speakers might sing about their mothers' nipples. In its rhythms, its wit and patterning, the poem becomes a game about language, a catalog of styles like fabric samples. It is as much, perhaps more, about *manners* of speech as about experience. Or, to extend more credit to the enterprise, the poem is about how perspective and style—that of the utopian versus the capitalist, for example—shape perception.

The passage is a lyric interlude in a longer meditative poem, but its medley of transformations is not so different from Wallace Stevens's "Thirteen Ways of Looking at a Blackbird." Hass's poem might be called "Thirteen Ways of Speaking of the Mother's Nipples." The field of the poetic fantasia is not experience but speech—a very specialized kind of experience. Hass's poem "performs" the anthropological idea that language shapes perception, that cultural givens create variations in consciousness. But "My Mother's Nipples" also is about how sophisticated we've become as readers—if a straightforward narrative is now considered too obvious or insufficiently challenging for a poet, an elliptical style like this one makes a sport for the postmodern skeptic. Whereas before, careful readers might have explicated the psychosymbolic implications of, say, a barn owl in a poem, they now can savor the structuralist wit of diction shifts.

Can a poem engage these self-conscious and detached linguistic strategies and handle content at the same time, in an enlightening way? Can a preoccupation with the artificiality of language combine itself with meaningful emotional ends? It's not clear how the new conventions will combine with the old agendas for art, but some poems demonstrate new territories of possibility.

One intriguing example of litany, and of New Poetry's relationship to style, gamesmanship, and representation is Thomas Sayers Ellis's poem "Or," a poem produced by a "system" of using words grouped around the syllable "or." Ellis's poem presents a radical strangeness: on the outside, it is a stylistically cryptic poem. Though it is tonally declarative, what is being declared is obscure; it doesn't use a single personal pronoun, or even much grammar. Impersonal, challenging, and ominous, "Or" is a broken text, as well as an example of a "procedural" poem. Its refusal of so many conventions implies that there is something fundamentally fragmented about language. The conventions that it invents, however, ultimately work to deliver content in a new way. Its *way* of saying has all kinds of productive implications about *what* it says:

> Or Oreo, or
> worse. Or ordinary.
> Or your choice
> of category
>
>   or
>   Color
>
> or any color
> other than Colored
> or Colored Only.
> Or "Of Color"
>
>   or
>   Other
>
> or theory or discourse
> or oral territory.

Oregon or Georgia
or Florida Zora

or
Opportunity

or born poor
or Corporate. Or Moor.
Or a Noir Orpheus
or Senghor

or
Diaspora . . .

"Or" is a list of names, a catalog of naming, but it is at first a mysterious list, opaque and disjunctive. It omits transitions, has not a single verb, offers neither narrative nor essayistic argument. The jumble of the poem is held in place by the repeating syllable, as well as frequent rhyme—these are the prosodic cohering agents of the erratic, dented, irregular dance in the litany. This list is not really a "progression"; its drama doesn't *escalate* except through repetition. The litany doesn't accrue a meaning that grows slowly in import and precision. Yet the poem has a powerful undertext of experience: the history and present of American racial estrangement.

In Ellis's poem, indirectness and tone (enigmatic, terse, challenging) provoke something like the itchy response we have to a riddle— *what is being talked about?* we want to know. Gradually, the dark subject matter oozes through the surface of these words; we sense the context and the content of the poem—racism—summoned up by this litany of fragments. The indirectness of the poem, its enigmatic stance, its randomness of signals (the way "born poor" and "Moor," "Yoruba" and "Electoral Corruption" cast an unevenly distributed net of inference) allow a menacing subtext to loom behind the poem. The poem is haunted by the multiple echoes and rhymes, by history and idiom. Here, our uncertainty, and our lack of intimacy with the speaker may create a more powerful effect than the conventions of clarity and intimacy.

Ellis's poem brings us to an important aesthetic crossroads: the intersection or interface between *representation, expression,* and *construction.* Ellis's poem is neither "organic" nor very "natural" in any conventional sense: it does not arise from a discernible story; its content does not seem to preexist its form. In fact, one of the sources of the poem's energy is that it neither entirely exists for its means nor its ends. Rather, they are commingled in the invention of the poem. At moments we might say the poem is making its way forward on the improvisation of the linguistic game; at times it is more emphatically asserting the referential urgency of its buried subject matter. Most excitingly perhaps, Ellis's poem suggests how a contemporary strategy of referential distortion can evoke and unlock a topic—racism— that has grown immune to the exhausted diction of conventional discourse.

Conclusion

In each of these poems, the act of naming is central, but a radical shift in poetic emphasis is visible, from the representational (paying homage to the cat Jeoffry) to the theatrical ingenuity of language (a *Kama Sutra* position called "Tiny Garden Hose"), to the tactile wit of language unhinged from function ("a dart is the jimmy of a limousine"), to the veiled, scrambled code words of a suppressed social history ("or Yoruba"). In each of these poems the act of naming is positioned in greater or lesser tension with the agenda of sense making, with the tense, inextinguishable desire for meaning. That dynamic dialectic (between sense and song) has always been a part of poetry, but recent American poetry is informed by new tensions, new understandings (the instability of language), and new possibilities. It shows no preference for narration, description, or confessions of the autobiographical self. It seizes hold of a radical plasticity in signification, and thus—as has been the case in other revolutions—poems of the new poetry head off in dozens of aesthetic directions.

These contemporary poets are diverse, but share some of the same fundamental characteristics: they have an instinct for gamesmanship; they are stylistically and technically intensive; their starting point is the innate *unanchoredness* of language (which can animate either affirmative or negative impulses). They feel the plasticity of language. They also feel an obligation to approach knowing in new, oblique ways. Not surprisingly, the old labels for such experiments—"experimental," "avant-garde," "LANGUAGE"—seem too encumbered with historical baggage to be useful. Better that they simply be called poets, or poems, of the New Poetry.

Poetic Housing:
Shifting Parts and Changing Wholes

Art is a house that tries to be haunted.

—EMILY DICKINSON

I

One of my fiction writer friends says that when he is working on a novel, his minor characters are always threatening to become major characters; and that his major character is always threatening to become a minor character. In other words, the process of story-telling is a seething, fermenting, somewhat unstable business. Such unwieldy shifts in proportion are also common, maybe even more common, in the making of poems—where a luminous image or statement can stage a coup d'état at any moment, disrupting the apparent agenda of the poem; where any digression can become more interesting than the main thematic line. It is often hard to keep the poetry train on the tracks, and the willfulness of doing so is often death to a poem. Art requires strange collaborations between decisiveness and surrender.

This constant threat of imbalance, of eruption, or potential amorphousness is especially present in the writing of free verse poetry. A sonneteer, or a writer of villanelles, has at least a preordained form to fill—to tell her roughly where the poem's beginning, middle, and end belong. But the free verse poet is always wondering about structure—guessing where the end of the poem might be, trying to detect what optimal dramatic shape might be emerging. This is why free verse poems, when not in the possession of a strong governing prosody, often seem, even if they are energetic and nutritious, somewhat sloppy.

Concise dramatic shape is important, even in "loose" associative poems, because poems are pressurized containers. A poem must contain energy, that is, hold it in. You can't carry water in a colander. And in order for the poem to contain, accumulate, and release pressure it must have a shape, a dramatic progression.

Let us liken a poem to an internal combustion engine. It is mounted, or housed, inside a sturdy frame. The structure must be sturdy because the contents of the poem are combustive; the vibrations are fierce. The housing contains and directs the explosive force of combustion with precision.

No doubt these principles apply to fiction and nonfiction as well as poetry. But structure is an especially crucial issue in poems. Why? Because poems have so few words, and occupy such a small physical space, the relative weight and function of words inside them can change very fast. Suddenly the theme turns out to be different than expected, or an image appears that is so resonant, it becomes indisputably structural. In general, odd proportions and pacing are more common and more acceptable in poetry. One need only think of Gertrude Stein's *Tender Buttons,* or to quote, in its entirety, a small poem by Robert Creeley, in which the semantic emphasis shifts with each line break:

> No way to
> tell you anything
> more than
> this one.

This unpredictability of poetry may be one reason why many so-called normal readers don't *read* poems—poems demand concentrated attention. They are full of misleadings, red herrings, carrots and sticks, ruses and wild goose chases, as well as great centrifugal centers.

Reading or listening to a poem is a play of prediction and uncertainty about where the prominences are, or the center is, about what will be the defining principles and components of the poem that is coming into view. During the whole of the poem-reading experience, we are scanning and reconfiguring, asking ourselves questions:

What kind of poem is this?

How big is the whole?

Where is the center? What is the central element?

Am I reading this for sound, sense, story, or image?
Is this image centrally significant?

What is the general perspective or tone?

What are the extraneous or secondary parts?

Here are two general but useful assertions:

1. Each of the lines and moments in a poem has a different degree of force and prominence; each moment has a relative weight, color, intensity, and sound. Some of these moments are, and must be, more important than others. In other words, poems are hierarchical.

2. As soon as we decide on primary moments, we can know what is secondary. Then, the secondary materials begin to orbit those primary moments in a supplementary role. The primary moments establish the contexts for the other moments. A poem can have more than one center of gravity, but it must have at least one.

To exemplify this orientation process, consider two poems by the French poet Jean Follain (1903–71), whose poems are marvelous little landscapes of rural life. In scale and housing, Follain's poems are especially rewarding of close study. They possess not only great charm but also the paradoxical quality of being economical and yet expansive; of being both calm and dynamic; of being naive yet worldly, soothing and yet surprisingly ruthless. One can learn a great deal about the principles that make poems work by studying these small machines. Here is Follain's "Signs for Travellers":

Travellers from the great spaces
when you see a girl
twisting in sumptuous hands
the black vastness of her hair
and when moreover
you see
near a dark baker's
a horse lying near death
by these signs you will know
that you have come among men.

"Signs for Travellers" is pretty clear in its shaping conceit. Using the rhetorical grammar of address, it presents itself as a Baedeker guide for a visitor from far away. *These,* the poem declares, *are the wonders of the world: a girl with big hair; a dying horse; a closed bakery.* Or, one might differently paraphrase: *beauty, youth, food, commerce, and death.* Or, one might summarize: *sensuality, mortality, simultaneity.*

The *housing* here, the operating premise and context of the poem, is the narrative occasion defined by the opening clause, whose tidy rhetorical triangle encompasses speaker, audience, and theme. The images in the poem, and their sequence, are important, of course, but they play a subordinate role; they furnish enrichment for the framing conceit. In "Signs for Travellers," the images don't become major characters. The major drama is the conceit itself, of a slideshow for extraterrestrials. The poem signifies the contextual primacy of this narrative in multiple ways. For instance the elevated, biblical-sounding inversion of line nine, "by these signs you will know," forcefully reiterates and develops the premise of travel guide. Also, perhaps, the use of the hyperbolic word *vastness* for the girl's hair communicates something contextual, implying that such hair is worth the intergalactic attention of a visitor. The context is: behold the wonders of the earth.

Nonetheless, even a small poem is as complex as a Swiss clock, full of pendulums and cogs. One fine, unobtrusive complexity that illustrates the characteristic interplay between housing, pressure, and con-

tents is the interesting discrepancy between the poem's first line and
its title: they are similar, yet subtly different; they overlap and modify
each other.

The first line of the poem conjures up an exotic *Twilight Zone* fiction narrative: *This is the world, earthling.* In contrast, the poem's title,
"Signs for Travellers," is more encompassing. "Signs for Travellers"
is *not* a greeting; rather, it suggests that the images in the poems are
not mere *things* but *signs.* Moreover, these omens are of significance
not just to *aliens* but to all travelers, a category that includes all of us
mortal pilgrims.

In this way, we can say that as a housing, the title enlarges the application of the poem to deeper, more universal, and more existential
implications. The premise of an address to outer space visitors may
have more exotic, grandiose flavor; but the title of Follain's poem has
more gravitas. And this discrepancy, doubling, or jostling between the
title and the first line is typical of how a poem works: we read and re-
read such a poem because its various resonances, nuances, and inflections reveal themselves to us successively.

II

A different Follain poem, "The Art of War," has a more fluid, shape-
shifting organization than "Signs for Travellers." As you read it, notice
how your impressionistic identification of context and contents, and
their relationships, keeps shifting:

> At the window a rose
> the colors of a blonde's young nipple.
> A mole walks underground.
> Peace, they say to the dog
> whose life is short.
> The air remains full of sunlight.
> Young men
> learn how to make war
> in order to redeem

a whole world they are told
but they still find the book
of theory unreadable.

So much adventure in a small space! Many details or moments
in this poem compete for primacy. As we read it, we wonder, which
is more crucial in the idiom of the poem: *nipples? roses? dog? peace?
kindness? remains?* Which details or images are *primary* (and therefore contextualizing), and which are *secondary?* What is the nucleus
around which all the other details orbit in supportive subordination?

The clue we look for is *relative weight:* the anchoring moment.
To my eyes, the dominating moment of "The Art of War," its gravita-
tional center, is identifiable by size and momentum, as the complex,
unfolding final sentence, the longest in the poem, with all its turns and
developments:

Young men
learn how to make war
in order to redeem
a whole world they are told
but they still find the book
of theory unreadable.

Follain's work in general is the quintessence of the associative mode,
which is to say, the relationships between its parts are largely loose and
inferential. Little is explicit, yet this last sentence in "The Art of War"
carries much of the intelligence of the poem. As the sentence unfolds
across line breaks, a chunk at a time, we watch the poem's stance complicate and shift. In syntax, lineation, and, not least, through meaning,
the sentence becomes crowded with complex relations: young men
act on the world, but they in turn are following the world's fallible,
perhaps unreadable instructions. We apprehend it all in a nimble second, recognizing and adjusting the parameters, deciding what the gist
of the poem is, the housing. Every other inflection of the poem turns
upon that structural recognition. The rose, the mole, the existence of

young women, and the short life of the dog are all bracketed within the contextualizing mortality of war.

But what, ultimately, does the omniscient speaker of Follain's poem suggest? What is being emphasized, among the interplay of these primary and secondary chords? Perhaps it is wisest here to be guided by tone. The tone in "The Art of War" might best be described as Sorrow, registered at a considerable philosophical distance. The narrating voice practices a simultaneous tenderness and detachment. One can see that a didactic potential lies readily within the poet's grasp—this could easily have been an antiwar poem—but that path is not chosen by the writer.

The interplay between any single detail of a poem and its whole shape is like the relationship between the string of a guitar and the resonating chamber behind it. The chamber of the whole is a background that catches and echoes back rich complications and integrations, timbre and poignancy and irony and depth.

One striking example of such interplay between a detail and the whole can be found in lines four and five: "Peace they say to the dog / whose life is short." Though seemingly quite different from the dominant sentence of the poem, these lines resonate with an innocent, slightly comic, relevance to the central spirit of the poem. If only half-consciously, we intuit the parallel between soldiers and dog; both are innocent, ignorant, and probably short-lived. Thus the blessing of dog by man seems poignant, prescient, and ignorant at once. It is a secondary moment that nonetheless substantially echoes and influences the whole, both reinforcing its center and enriching its tone.

As in our previous example, the poem's title, "The Art of War," strikes a note distinct from the text of the poem. The phrase "the art of war" asserts a sophisticated, ironic tone not audible in the text of the poem, a perspective in quiet tension with that text. Though it may not be the frame of the poem, the title nonetheless adds its dialectical perspective.

What if a friendly reader rearranged Follain's poem to straighten out its odd kinks and "irregularities," as you yourself might, if this were your poem and you were following workshop advice about clarification?

What if our goal were to make the poem more unified and less ambiguous in its emphasis? Seeking to clarify its emphasis, one might cut and paste a little, and arrive at something like the following:

Why I Grow Flowers
The air remains full of sunlight.
A mole walks underground.
Young men
learn how to make war
in order to redeem
a whole world.
Peace they say to the dog
whose life is short.
At the window a rose
the color of a blonde's young nipple.

Rebuilt, the poem now has a quite different thrust. This version emphasizes the pleasures of peace, and seems to infer some sound reasons for applying for conscientious objector status. After all, it concludes with palpable arguments for peace: a flower garden and the promise of erotic adventure. This revision is distinctly more unified than the original. It retains a faint irony in the third sentence. Yet, unfortunately, "Why I Grow Flowers" is a less dynamic and less interesting poem than "The Art of War." Loose as it still is, and not without nuance, this version is a lesser poem.

Though inferior, this shuffle and reorganization, this turning up and down of volume, inflection and motif, are more or less what we do, are they not, every time we write a poem? In revision, we are seeking a dramatic shape, for the best poem among several poems. We are hunting it to haunt it.

Such is the dialectic of parts and wholes, and the difference between competence and ambitiousness, between tidiness and dynamic vision, between a declarative artist or a more intuitive one. All the agencies of sensibility are brought to bear in a collaboration of word

choices, arrangements, timing, suppressions, additions, and syntactical choices.

III

To reiterate: poems have centers of gravity, and complex internal
structures. Apollinaire coined a term, "the internal frame," to describe
the way a single internal detail—be it tone or image or statement—
can serve as the context, center, or organizing principle of a poem.

My examples, drawn from Follain, might suggest that a loose structure is the most dynamic for the reader and writer. Follain's poems
have hidden coherences, elements of distraction and misdirection or
obliquity. Part of their charm is their erratic quality. When elements
are loosely conjoined and available for reshufflings of understanding, a high degree of skillful responsiveness is elicited from the reader.
Follain's poems, so representative of the associative poetic tradition,
would suggest that such poems *can* be more participatory and exciting
for the reader.

Yet "looseness" is a tricky business in aesthetics, and a writer in
an excited state of composition can easily misjudge the degree of
coherence in the connect-the-dots mode. Without a firm commitment to a particular emphasis, the poem may suffer the vagueness of
undercontextualization. Consider Lesle Lewis's "Shooting the Bear," a
contemporary poem that seems to bargain in the energy of unstated
connections:

> Like the novel in verse, the novel in verse, dogs in this town
>   drive cars.
>
> Houses expose themselves slowly.
>
> It's flammable linseed oil to which the cabinetmaker who
>   made our
> feeders after losing his fingers loses his shop.

We must think of the little nun's happiness.

If we shoot the bear, it won't bother the feeders.

The birds love our willow trees, and love *is* the word.

What holds "Shooting the Bear" together, and is it held together enough? Anecdote? Whimsical tone? Lyric intelligence? As previously, we look for a moment or an element that is primary, that serves as an emphasis around which the other moments are arranged supportively. We look for a housing.

The best candidate for centrality in "Shooting the Bear" is the complex third sentence, which contains the most story and is grammatically staged in the most interesting way. This compact tale of a cabinetmaker possesses the feel of a parable, one that might provide the key to the gestalt of the entire poem.

The syntax of this sentence is staged in a way that feels significant and intentional. With some effort, we can sort out the narrative information, but the result seems aimless, placing the emphasis on *linseed oil* rather than *cabinetmaker*. Sentence three is grammatically odd, but its oddity does not clarify or strategically assert a primary understanding. If we try to relate it to the preceding and subsequent lines, we are still left scratching our heads. What relationship does the linseed oil fire have to the little nun's happiness, or to the car-driving dogs in this town? Dimly in the background, like a distant bell, seems to lie a thesis that life requires choices and includes damage—but it is a faint chime.

If we can't identify a center of gravity here, around which other elements can organize themselves supplementally, then we are in the presence of a democracy, but not a poem. In reading "Shooting the Bear," we taste the excitement of suspense, but not the gratification of arrival. Ultimately, we have only the mystique of mystification. We may appreciate the pleasure of an eccentric mind at work, or a curious style, but not the way that style is recognizably a resourceful response to experience.

"Shooting the Bear" is representative of a certain strain of contemporary American poetry, an aesthetic whose idea of art is to withhold context. The idea is to cultivate the pleasure of elusiveness, which is close to the pleasure of mystery. But there is a difference between elusiveness and evasiveness, and between mystery and obfuscation. Such a poem may seem generous for its inclusion of quite diverse contents—yet it does not *enclose* them; it does not house or contain them in a precise and directive way. Therefore, it does not gather or contain power.

In contemporary poetry, the surface of Association and the surface of Disassociation can look very much alike. Associative thinking arises from delight about the way things go together. Disassociative poetry arises from an emphasis on how things do not connect. The difference between "Shooting the Bear" and "The Art of War" is that Follain's poem skillfully evokes the proportions and the causalities inherent in experience; it makes us think about the way the world fits together, and rewards us for doing so.

In contrast, "Shooting the Bear" is a bemused mirage of a poem. It projects a confidence that seems plausible, but when we follow the clues, we are not rewarded by more understanding. And, we must remember, poetry is not a faith-based charity. No artful housing means no containment of energy, no portability, no accumulating pressure, and therefore no shelf life. What energy is here will leak away quickly. It is a remarkable fact that a style of poetry can have a temporary charisma, which lasts awhile but then dissipates and vanishes when the cultural circumstances, or the neurological moment, passes.

IV

In contrast to the loose associative constructions of Follain, Eavan Boland's poem "The Parcel" is a masterfully precise and complexly hierarchichal poem that offers many useful lessons about the relation between details and housing. "The Parcel" is authoritative in how it handles primary and secondary elements, and rich in how it balances forward momentum and sideways enrichment. It contains intellectual work as well as personal emotional coloration and emphasis:

There are dying arts and
one of them is
the way my mother used to make up a parcel.
Paper first. Mid-brown and coarse-grained as wood.
The worst sort for covering a Latin book neatly
or laying flat at Christmas on a pudding bowl.
It was a big cylinder. She snipped it open
and it unrolled quickly across the floor.
All business, all distance.
Then the scissors.
Not a glittering let-up but a dour
pair, black thumb-holes,
the shears themselves the colour of the rained-
on steps a man with a grindstone climbed up
in the season of lilac and snapdragon
and stood there arguing the rate for
sharpening the lawnmower and the garden pair
and this one. All-in.
The ball of twine was coarsely braided
and only a shade less yellow than
the flame she held under the blunt
end of the sealing-wax until
it melted and spread into a brittle
terracotta medal.
Her hair dishevelled, her tongue between her teeth,
she wrote the address in the quarters
twine had divided the surface into.
Names and places. Crayon and fountain-pen.
The town underlined once. The country twice.
It's ready for the post
she would say and if we want to know
where it went to—
a craft lost before we missed it—watch it go
into the burlap sack for collection.
See it disappear. Say

this is how it died
out: among doomed steamships and out-dated trains,
the tracks for them disappearing before our eyes,
next to station names we can't remember
on a continent we no longer
recognise. The sealing-wax cracking.
The twine unravelling. The destination illegible.

One can feel how concerted, which is to say, how *concert-like* the forward movement of this poem is, how concise and coordinated in every dimension, and yet how rich the relationships are between its parts.

One of the most interesting aspects is how the poem opens. "The Parcel" is largely a poem of personal memory, yet Boland uses a discursive premise, or envelope, in which to wrap that narrative. "There are dying arts," she says, imposing a panoramic and sociological frame around the poem, "and one of them is / the way my mother used to make up a parcel."

It is the kind of decision we all make when we are beginning a poem. Yet how much depends upon that first step! The stakes become more evident if one considers what the opening would sound like if Boland had begun narratively rather than discursively, say, with the sentence, "My mother used to make up a parcel."

What is the motive for this opening strategy? The answer is pretty clear: the poet wishes to resist autobiographical sentimentality; she wishes to control the flow of emotion. For a poet like Boland, with a very controlled temperament, this is a brilliant choice, one that counterweights passion with intellectual reserve. This opening also has an amplifying effect on the scale and housing of the poem; the framework is officially not "my family story" but the notion of "dying arts."

The opening is not the only way in which emotion is curbed in "The Parcel." Another technique of restraint is visible in the poet's recurrent use of terse grammatical fragments: "Paper first. Mid-brown and coarse-grained as wood. / The worst sort for covering a Latin book neatly." Such curt units of speech, with no pronoun attached to them, disguise and restrain the pressure of personal feeling that might overflow a more expressive grammar.

Another marvelous instance of complex relations between housing and details in "The Parcel" is to be found in Boland's athletic use of metaphor. Often, substantial amounts of narrative are smuggled or enveloped inside an extended figurative passage, like the one that begins in line ten: "Then the scissors. / . . . the shears themselves the colour of the rained- / on steps a man with a grindstone climbed up / in the season of lilac and snapdragon / and stood there arguing the rate for / sharpening the lawnmower and the garden pair / and this one."

Even in the middle of a sentence, complex relations exist between packages and contents. Reading this passage is like a roller-coaster ride, and it demands of us, and rewards us for doing, all the complex work of going back and forth between part and whole. Boland exerts the same skill two lines later, when she describes the ball of twine as

> . . . only a shade less yellow than
> the flame she held under the blunt
> end of the sealing-wax until
> it melted and spread into a brittle
> terracotta medal.

Every distinctive poet has a particular, peculiar way of putting things together, of constructing relations of subordination and dominance, and Boland's metaphorical virtuosity is one example. The hierarchies through which we view the world are perceptual, grammatical, and metaphorical. We each do it in our own way. Ultimately, such devices and habits are what constitute sensibility.

For all its restraint, "The Parcel" has unmistakably intimate points of emotion: "It's ready for the post / she would say," and we are alive to the scene, as we are present for the vision of the mother's tongue between her concentrating teeth. These are emotionally charged moments, but they are spare and undramatized in presentation; moreover, they are embedded in the surface of a much more objective, cool narration.

In the conclusion of "The Parcel," the poet chooses to dilate and

enlarge the perspective of the poem once more (as she did at its beginning), making her subject much larger than one person's personal loss.
Thus, "The Parcel" becomes an elegy for the past and for the future,
which has lost such tactile intimacy with things and places. The poem
is an elegy in which personal and collective loss are joined in a way
that they richly augment each other.

We might call the personal anecdotes in "The Parcel" *subsets* of the
whole. All poems have subsets; as long as the relationship between the
elements and the whole of the poem is clear, such subsets can contain
vast, deep materials. This too is a matter of hierarchy, whether the relation between parts is loosely implied or tightly constructed by grammar. One can do very worthwhile things in a subset of a poem.

V

Another way to describe the purpose of effective housing is to say that
any poem should hold up its best moment to its greatest advantage.
If you cannot recognize the best moment of your draft and position
it, you risk obscuring your primary treasure among a lot of other effects. You will make a muddy poem. Thus, to design a good housing
is essential.

Anne Carson's "God's List of Liquids" offers one final example
of the infinite athleticism with which contents and contexts are constantly reorganizing themselves within a poem. Carson's poem, to uti-
lize our terminology, has several centers of gravity and several shifting
contexts; yet they coexist in conversation, and somehow don't trip
over each other. Here is the poem:

> It was a November night of wind.
> Leaves tore past the window.
> God had the book of life open at PLEASURE
>
> and was holding the pages down with one hand
> because of the wind at the door.
> *For I made their flesh as a sieve*

wrote God at the top of the page
And then listed in order:
Alcohol
Blood
Gratitude
Memory
Semen
Song
Tears
Time.

Carson's poem begins with the great convenience offered by narrative frame: God has a book in November. Within that fabular frame we get three contexts: *pleasure, liquids,* and *sieve.* The book of life is opened to the page of pleasure. And a list of liquids is central, as presented in the title. One more influential concept is elicited by the italicized phrase *"For I made their flesh as a sieve."* The human body therefore is defined as something that liquids flow through. As we read Carson's poem, and get to the list of "substances," we are tasked with collating and coordinating each item in terms of these three presiding contexts: *liquids, pleasure, sieve.*

The device of the list is a fairly primitive literary form on its own, primitive because it is not subject to any grammar except sequence. But in Carson's poem, the list functions richly and complexly because of the surrounding contexts, and the irregular ways in which the list items conform or don't conform to our expectations. While a reader works through the list, he is scrambling to contextualize the items—*"Alcohol / Blood / Gratitude."* The unlikeness of the items on the list makes this an adventure between contents and contexts, wholes and parts, backgrounds and foregrounds. As we go on correlating and collating, as the list expands conceptually to include more dimensions of the human condition than we might have expected *("Memory / Tears / Time"),* we are also involved in a drama of escalating poignancy and implication. The last few items on the list amount to a climax—*Tears* and *Time.* Song, tears, and time are all, we understand, liquids, and all, we must acknowledge, are forms of pleasure, all of which, we understand, pass through us. We are thus brought, in a very tactile way, to the realization that we cannot hold anything.

The radical interplay between details and contexts, between housing and items, and the constant reorganizing that "God's List of Liquids" provokes us to do is complex yet perfectly lucid. This is the kind of dramatic power that can be achieved formally, if a poet is ruthless and attentive to structures and priorities. Such ingenious, surprising poems are a perpetual motivation to keep keen our ambition to learn and to discover new ways to construct our poems.

◇ ◇ ◇ ◇ ◇

Facts and Feelings:
Information, Layering,
and the Composite Poem

For to exist on the earth is beyond any power to name.

—CZESLAW MILOSZ

At one time, even before writing existed, poetry was a repository for knowledge—not just stories of battle, love, and national identity, but of practical things, like how to break a horse or how to raise honeybees. Virgil, in Book 4 of his *Georgics,* will still tell you where to place your beehives (under a shady tree, near fresh water); he will describe to you the distinct social roles in bee society, and tell you how to heal your bees when they are sick and listless:

> Since life has brought the same misfortunes to bees as ourselves,
> if their bodies are weakened with wretched disease,
> you can recognize it straight away by clear signs:
> as they sicken their color immediately changes: a rough
> leanness mars their appearance: then they carry outdoors
> the bodies of those without life, and lead the sad funeral
>   procession:
> or else they hang from the threshold linked by their feet, or linger
> indoors, all listless with hunger and dull with depressing cold.
> . . . .
> Then I'd urge you to burn fragrant resin, right away,
> and give them honey through reed pipes, freely calling them
> and exhorting the weary insects to eat their familiar food.

It's good too to blend a taste of pounded oak-apples
with dry rose petals, or rich new wine boiled down
over a strong flame, or dried grapes from Psithian vines,
with Attic thyme and strong-smelling centaury.
                ("Disease in Bees," trans. A. S. Kline, lines 251–58, 263–69)

Information and poetry have had a long, sometimes ambivalent relationship. It was probably the romantic movement in particular, in the nineteenth century, that pushed information toward the margin of poetry, and replaced it, or displaced it, with sensibility and inspiration. Blame Coleridge, who allocated fact checking and memory to the inferior poetic category of Fancy. Poetry, as Coleridge said, does not *record* or *describe* the material realm, but transforms it. Though some efforts in the twentieth century have run counter to that trend, we still can feel, in contemporary poetry, the consequence of the prejudice. When inner life is privileged over facticity, the representation of outer life recedes to the periphery, or disappears; fact and its physics, and even its vocabulary, become the property of scientists, economists, and carpenters. For the romantics, and their many aesthetic progeny—the Confessionals, the Beats, the New York poets, the Deep Imagists, among others—it was feelings, not facts, that counted.

In contemporary poetry, despite all our postmodern skepticisms about the self, the poetic emphasis on personal subjectivity remains strong—as well it should. After all, who will stand up for the nobility of inner life if not poetry? Not reality TV. Take the brassy subjectivity of Dorothea Lasky, in her plaintive yet strangely convincing poem "Everyone Keeps Me from My Destiny":

Everyone keeps me from my destiny
Keeps me from it
And keeps me locked away from beauty
And they can't feel my beauty
In me reaching out
Like glass into itself
And then into glass

And everyone keeps me from myself
Cause the self they had imagined
Was flesh and bone
And this flesh I am is glass
And everyone keeps me from my genius
Because genius is not human
And everyone wants me to be human
And I am not human
And everyone expects me to be something they are,
which is human
And I can't be anything they are which is human
Because I am not human
And they are
And I am not human

Lasky's poem avidly channels the primal subjective self. It contains almost no reference to the objective world. Yet it convinces through its emotional forcefulness, and through our sense of the poem's genuine source in the fiery element of identity.

Poetry and Information

Locating the poetry in worldly information, and locating worldly information inside poems, might not be easy, but if contemporary poetry is to claim the status of ongoing relevance, it must interest itself in the stuff of mortgage crisis, insurgency sponsorship, and lithium batteries. In seclusion, American poetry is ever liable to become the production of psychobiography and wisdom statements. Or, on the other hand, to become an asylum of insular aesthetics and hyper-intellectual jargons, wielded by poetry nerds.

The challenge of inclusiveness is complicated by plenty of factors. Our age is characterized by a constancy, diversity, and immensity of data that have never before been encountered. Even to contemplate the scope of modern information is overwhelming. When the world is too big to see or understand, how does one make an inclusive poem?

When so many things are happening simultaneously, how can a poem or a work of fiction convey the way it *feels* to be an individual human consciousness? Wholesale exclusion of the world almost seems a necessary first reflex for the making of art. Given such an environment, one can see why many poets would prefer the segregated terrain of the subjective.

Moreover, our sense of our own cognitive limitations has never been so acute. Increasingly, we recognize randomness rather than causality as a governing principle in life, fortune, and experience. We are more aware than ever how our cognition, perception, and emotional lives are prejudiced and shaped by systems in whose design we have had no part—economic systems, ideological systems, linguistic systems. In our time, information is no longer simply information—it is always inflected by the manners of its presentation. Even to claim that the world is "knowable" can seem like a grandiosity. And how is poetry to include its own fallibility?

And yet, our poetic responsibility to reality—to what Czeslaw Milosz has named "the passionate pursuit of reality"—persists. As a poet and a person, I want to include both Lyme disease and moonlight in my poems. I want economics and racial reality and bootleg pharmaceutical companies in India. I want reggae music coming out of the perforated speakers on the gas pump, while a block away, a twenty-nine-year-old paralegal reads the result of her pregnancy test and rolls her eyes in disbelief. I value art that looks outward as well as inward, that sees the world cross-eyed as well as through a cold eye. I want to include a world larger than that of my personal experience.

But how can a poem manage and orchestrate it all?

How can I get this ship into that bottle?

The Test-Tube Paradigm

One helpful thought experiment is to visualize the poem as a kind of test tube, or terrarium, into which the poet allows a limited but generously diverse sample of the world. This data sample should have something *unedited* and wild about it in terms of selection—but not so much *quantity* that its plenitude overwhelms the poem. Once that data is inside the glass container of the poem, says the poet, let us see if we can orchestrate it, if we can arrange it into the poignant suite of harmonics and disharmonies that we call a poem.

The hazards are clear. If the poet allows in too *much* information, or too big an information sample, then she may be showcasing an abundance that verges on shapelessness. If the poet allows too *little* data, or too little disorder, into the test tube, she is running a rigged game, an arrangement with a fixed outcome. Such a poet is in danger of writing the same poem again and again, like a laboratory that makes the same discovery year after year.

Modernism itself was an artistic revolution conceived in part to handle the surfeit and swirl of the twentieth century. Eliot's *The Waste Land,* Pound's *Cantos,* Gertrude Stein's circularity, Berryman's *Dream Songs:* new forms arise when existing modes no longer seem to be adequately keeping up with reality, experience, and our age.

If one considers the sorts of technique that have appealed most to literary writers and readers in the last century—fracture, collage, abcedarium poems, poems that flirt with sampling and randomness, or Oulipo techniques—we can recognize how craft has been attempting to keep up with the Information Problem, to accommodate a reality in which more data, more speed, and less fixity have been evident. If these are the parameters of contemporary experience, it is no wonder modern aesthetics have gravitated toward collagist, typed-over, fragmentary, skewed artistic forms.

"The most impressive systems," said the evolutionary scientist Stephen Jay Gould, "are the ones that incorporate the greatest amount of the world's dazzling disorder." Yet implicit in Gould's statement is the premise that such ambitious systems also retain a *structure.* Can realism and introspective poetics coexist inside the same poem? Can facts and feelings? Worldliness and subjectivity? Must we choose, as poets? One especially ambitious formal strategy for handling manifold reality is the composite poem.

Characteristics of the Composite Poem

The composite poem approaches the real through an aesthetic process of sampling, counterpoint, and dialectic. It has a desire for inclusiveness—yet, knowing that actual inclusiveness is impossible, it gathers a harmonic of unlike things into its landscape. Here are some of its features.

1. The composite poem likes information. It incorporates data from an array of realms—history, science, economics, politics, personal life, and news. Such data serves as counterweight to the powerful convention of the personal and subjective in the recent history of poetry. By counterpointing facts, styles, and information systems, the realms of the external and internal reality *haunt* each other in the composite poem. In Tomas Tranströmer's work, for instance, we find economic insights juxtaposed with existential angst, juxtaposed with the tender and precise observations of a naturalist.

2. The composite poem aims to capture the irregular character of experience, its lopsidedness and illogic. It is disproportionate and disheveled by design, as a way of making it difficult to align with a reductive meaning. Likewise, the composite poem also often nods to the imprecisions, limitations, and difficulties of mimesis, and to the influence of language and ideological systems for how they affect our vision. Toward that end, it mixes notes of tragedy, whimsy, indifference, and cheerfulness.

3. The composite poem sometimes has a relative tonal impersonality, offering an appearance of detachment. Or perhaps it is more true to say that it contains simultaneous levels of detachment and attachment.

4. The composite poem thus avoids one prominent liability of the romantic temperament: it refuses the paradigm of a singular heroic speaker who occupies the center of the poetic monologue. Instead, it brings together diverse voices and sources, which exist in counterpoint and collectively create a "field" of knowing. The poetic center might be built around a place or a motif rather than a single self.

5. Unsurprisingly, perhaps, when the composite poem fails, it might be from an overindulgence of randomness. Similarly, it may be susceptible to a lack of progression or to passivity. Because its parts are free floating and more or less discrete, they may seem self-sufficient or merely fragmentary. Ideally, however, the parts must complicate and activate each other. They must resonate dynamically.

Reece: Diverse Data

The composite poetic method can be found on display in the "Florida Ghazals" of Spencer Reece. Reece combines samples of worldly information alongside passionate testimonies to subjective life. Using the free-floating, capsule-like couplets of the ghazal form, Reece arranges errant materials selectively. The resulting counterpoint is satisfyingly crisp and convincing:

> Down here, the sun clings to the earth and there is no darkness.
> Down here, the silence of the sea and the silence of the swamp
>   seep into our muscles.
>
> All night Dolores labors between the sea grapes and the empty
>   park.
> Our town prostitute, she listens for a long time. Her listening
>   makes her strong.
>
> The teenage boy locks his door and combs the obscene magazine.
> His calloused left hand chops the gloss in waves. The silence of
>   the naked ladies builds.
>
> The Cape Sable seaside sparrows' population dropped 25 percent.
>   Females are silent.
> Male calls are counter and multiplied by sixteen: this is how we
>   track what cannot be seen.
>   . . . .

Egas Moniz wins the Nobel Prize in 1949 for pioneering
   lobotomies.
I am a pioneer of silence but the silencing of madness haunts
   me because it is unresolved.

By layering and juxtaposing data from different arenas, and by
shifting between private and public narratives, Reece sets up complex
strata and resonances of representation. Here the factual data validates
the speaker's credibility, as well as providing subtle analogues to the
speaker's inner life. The result is a poetry more capacious and poly-
valent than either a sheerly personal "subjective poem" or a purely
"reportorial" poem. Here is a poetic in which information and private
life haunt each other.

Take, for example, the oddly factual couplet regarding sparrow
populations in Cape Sable. We are told how the data about males
and females is gathered; one gender, we learn, the female, is silent.
The existing population of that gender is extrapolated from the
number of male sparrow calls. This information, layered alongside
the peopled vignettes of the poem—the teenage boy who mastur-
bates, the town prostitute who works the park—infiltrates the poem
with a nuanced atmosphere of loneliness. We recognize the loneliness of sexuality itself—especially in this place, where one is only
counted by being invisible and absent. Similarly, the first-person
narrator of the poem, who only appears in the poem's final line, is, he
says, "a pioneer of silence." This intimate testimony is layered alongside another piece of "data" from the public world, the invention of
the lobotomy. Collating these episodic sentences and couplets, we
can recognize a gathering host of complex, nuanced patterns in this
troubled world.

Through layering and triangulation, Reece's ghazal achieves a
deeper, more capacious relationship to the real. The composite poem
alloys chunks, bits, and bytes of the objective and the subjective into
a loose kind of composition—one whose hybrid roughness does not
smooth out the heterogeneity of the real, but nonetheless seeks to

harmonically organize it, to arrange it into a credible, believably disorganized form.

Reece's poem is representative of the composite method in other ways as well. His ghazal appears to take a *place,* Florida, as its central focus, rather than a personal story; this choice allows the poem to assemble diverse voices and sources that exist in counterpoint, and collectively create a "field" of sensibilities. The composite poem thus avoids one pitfall of the romantic temperament: it refuses the paradigm of the singular heroic speaker.

By such strategies, perhaps it *is* possible to have it both ways: to infuse the poem with the credibility, textural wealth, and fascination of worldly data, and also to delve deep into the precincts of the soul.

Labeling such poetics is difficult. "Florida Ghazal" might be called a "collage," and yet it's not, quite—the juxtapositions are not violent or abrupt. Reece's poetic method could also be tagged with the label of "associative imagination," and yet that doesn't seem quite accurate either, for Reece's technique is one of overlay and simultaneity, of stratification, rather than of a mind leaping forward from point to point.

The Self Also Can Be Portrayed as a Composite

Anne Carson's short poem "Strange Hour (Outcast Hour)" demonstrates that composite techniques can be used as well to present selfhood in a manner that is more encompassing than the conventional. Like Reece, Carson is deft at collaging and blending, fusing and juxtaposing data and selfhoods. Her poems collate outer and inner realms, contradictory sensations and thoughts, feeling and perception; the result is an evocative array of dimensions, which are at once fragmentary and inclusive. "Strange Hour" is an especially economical but layered example.

Because the poem is narrated by one speaker, and is largely scenic, it might initially appear to be staged in a rather conventional poetic mode. But closer inspection reveals some oddities of composition that add unexpected registers and angles to its lyric psychological portrait:

3 A.M. cool palace roar of Oakland night.
Not even a siren then a siren far off.
Train passed a while ago now nothing.

Bare lightbulb in garage across the street who left it on.

Every sentence should contain a fact at least.
No one but myself ever seems to set foot on this balcony
strange to say.
Undertone of hatred I cannot eliminate
from my feelings of friendship for most people.
Clear at this hour.

"Strange Hour" is, on first encounter, a quiet urban lyric—a compact, largely descriptive poem that might be likened to a longish haiku.
But though the poem offers a unified scene, its special compressed ra-
diance arises from its unusual composite of three (at least) distinct
layers of consciousness and data: precise perceptual information, linguistic self-consciousness, and a terse, almost dislocated report from
the interior emotive self.

Carson's first two stanzas are austere, intimate, and observant.
These four quiet lines record external data unobtrusively filtered by
a solitary receiving consciousness, in a voice so unself-conscious in
register that it forgoes personal pronouns. This intimate moment is
interrupted at the exact middle of the poem, in line five, by a sudden,
solitary admonition about the act of writing: a declaration of aesthetic
principle very consistent with the theme of this essay:

Every sentence should contain a fact at least.

Abruptly, the poem's pastoral illusion is disintegrated. Although
this single end-stopped line is attached to stanza three, it arrives seemingly out of nowhere, and its subject matter ("What Are the Rules for
Making a Poem?") is not developed in any subsequent lines. This in-

serted idea belongs to a different, one could say, neural category than what precedes and what follows. Yet we accept it, because (a) it is interesting; (b) it complicates our notion of what a poem is, what this poem is, and who the speaker is; and (c) its appearance is so brief. In short, as readers, we are willing to tolerate considerable inconsistency, especially if the result is a rewarding complexity.

After the speaker's aesthetic endorsement of the factual world, the first self-reference to the physical presence of the observer appears: "No one but myself ever seems to set foot on this balcony," she says. And then—again, abruptly—a revelation spikes through, in fragment form, as if torn off the flank of the inner life.

> Undertone of hatred I cannot eliminate
> from my feelings of friendship for most people.

This sentence fragment delivers an incongruously intense piece of private confession. Hatred is a strong emotion, and "most people" is a lot of people. It is a startling exclamation—one that has had no preparation in the poem, and one that receives no development after its appearance. These "extraneous" moments provocatively strain the seams of the lyric container. Yet consequently, they distort and enlarge the poem into something more mysterious, more alert, and beautiful than it would otherwise be. In another more "romantic" kind of poem, the revelation of hatred would beg exploration, and transformation. In the composite poem, even a charged subjective "declaration" possesses the status of only one objective fact among others "clear at this hour."

In its use of disparate angularities, Carson's soliloquy presents an unconventional, stratified vision of the self, one that implies that a world in which the material and spiritual, the inner and outer, the perceptual and the linguistic coexist, yet do not entirely match up. Human nature inhabits multiple worlds nonexclusively, simultaneously, and discontinuously. Such a version of the self may be less unified in its presentation, but poetically more trustworthy than the average confessional poem, which tends to operate entirely within the psychological realm. As a result the poem slips free of its pastoral identity, and it becomes that much more intriguingly, complexly contemporary.

The composite poem is not driven by cause and effect; does not arise from antecedent, nor spawn consequence. It does not insist on conflict; it creates spaciousness through variety, and through an implicit assertion of coexistence.

The Composite Poem as a Reprieve from Narcissism

Robert Hass is one of the best contemporary practitioners of the composite mode. Hass also understands the tonic, contrapuntal value of data in a poem that might be otherwise entirely psychological or narrative. "August Notebook," a multisectioned, multifaceted poem about the death of a brother, deploys the tempering effect of information upon subjectivity. Aside from the sheer pleasures of facticity, a brief, midpoem sociological lecture by the speaker provides a place in which to stand free of sentiment, and free from the habit of psychologizing that sometimes seems to dog the American poem:

> Because I woke again thinking of my brother's body
> and why anyone would care in some future
> that poetry addresses how a body is transferred
> from the medical examiner's office,
> which is organized by local government
> and issues a certificate establishing that the person
> in question is in fact dead and names the cause
> or causes, to the mortuary or cremation society,
> most of which are privately owned businesses
> and run for profit and until recently tended
> to be family businesses with skills and decorums
> passed from father to son, and often quite ethnically
> specific, in a country like ours made from crossers
> of borders, as if, in the intimacy of death,
> some tribal shame or squeamishness or sense

> of propriety asserted itself so that the Irish
> buried the Irish and the Italians the Italians.
> In the south in the early years of the last century
> it was the one business in which a black person
> could grow wealthy and pass on a trade
> and a modicum of independence to his children.
> I know this because Judith wrote a piece about it. . . .

In a poem necessarily addressed to personal loss, this sociological digression acts to freshen the air before a return to grief. A poem is "the cry of an occasion," but that occasion, we are reminded, is infiltrated by manifold contexts—economic, civic, historical, racial. If invoked skillfully, such data can save a poetic occasion from easy sentimentality, or, alternatively, can deepen our recognition of how every story extends in many human directions. In this passage, with its ostensibly sociological register of voice, we are made aware of how even the most personal moment is touched, backstage, by commerce, history, tribalism, and all the ironic byways to dignity. Pathos and struggle, it turns out, are stacked in all quarters of the world.

Moreover, through this curious digression, the speaker is relieved of a different, potentially costly freight—the appearance of self-absorption, and the grandiose presumption of the self's uniqueness.

Tranströmer: The Power of Disarray

One of the most masterful poetic dialecticians of the twentieth century is Tomas Tranströmer—his poems accommodate many octaves and chord changes in their range. He "layers" and conglomerates the spiritual and the informational, the existential and the scientific, the narrative and lyrical into his poems. He smuggles and camouflages his significations inside a broad variety of methods. The poems that result are almost subliminal fields of understanding, fields in which insight, experience, and ignorance coexist comfortably with precision.

Here's an example of a composite poem by Tranströmer:

Oklahoma

I

The train stalled far to the south. Snow in New York,
but here we could go in shirtsleeves all night.
Yet no one was out. Only the cars
sped by in flashes of light like flying saucers.

II

"We battlegrounds are proud
of our many dead . . ."
said a voice as I awakened.

The man behind the counter said:
"I'm not trying to sell anything,
I'm not trying to sell anything,
I just want to show you something."
And he displayed the Indian axes.

The boy said:
"I know I have a prejudice,
I don't want to have it, sir.
What do you think of us?"

III

This motel is a foreign shell. With a rented car
(like a big white servant outside the door).
Nearly devoid of memory, and without profession,
I let myself sink to my midpoint.

                                        Trans. May Swenson

What a strange poem "Oklahoma" is. Tranströmer presents its
mysterious parts without assembly instructions, and without any
overarching statement that would divulge a secret order. Imagine
how convenient it would be, for example, to have a title like "History"
placed over this poem—a single idea that would lock the poem into

a thematic framework; that would be more directive and *determinate,* thus saving us a lot of uncertainty about the shape and the disposition of this diverse data.

Instead, the segments of "Oklahoma" conjure up an ambiguous atmosphere in which various narratives are suspended, like particles. The relationship between these particles is neither linear nor hierarchical. The poem's overall tone is studiedly neutral, and the lack of connective language, transitions, or mediation between the poem's parts is notable.

Consider the rather amorphous middle section of the poem. What are these various floating "voices"? Fragmentary speeches that seem to issue, respectively, from a battleground graveyard, a boy, a merchant of Native American relics? In the context of the poem's title, "Oklahoma," they might be heard as the various voices of a place. We might go further and say they are the spectral voices of commerce, history, and anxiety, expressing themselves equally; all injuries of the past that persist into the present. The poem itself is a constellation, a field of impressions about a place—Oklahoma. But what an odd, nonlogical and nondiscursive form in which to present these inflected impressions.

I don't think Yeats would have extended much credibility to this poem. "Oklahoma" doesn't exert power in the romantic sense of great verbal music, nor in the gathering energy of rhetoric. It doesn't possess a heroic mounting cadence, nor does it plant a flag of beauty or truth on top of Mount Experience. It doesn't conquer anything. The poem's claim to unity could be called sketchy. Even its principal speaker is indistinct, and near-anonymous.

And yet, Tranströmer's poem feels quite real to me. "Oklahoma" emanates a quality of *mystery,* without the taint of intentional mystification or coy elusiveness. Its poetic form feels adequate to the flavor of the modern condition. Undeniably, the risk the poet assumes with such a nondirective form is an appearance of passivity, or noncommittalness. Yet the poem's reserve comes through as a register of modesty, even of soulful maturity. We sense an integrity, that is, an underlying structure beneath the poem's fragmentary surface.

Tranströmer's poem also unobtrusively carries, in its ambient way, many different *kinds* of information—kinds of information that would not ordinarily occupy the same plane of poetic consciousness. The ghost voice of battlegrounds, the soulless commercialism of merchants, the guilt of self-consciousness. The speaker himself is more than a witness, or innocent bystander; he has a car like "a big white servant" outside his door; one can hear the jingling chains of association attached to that description—inferences about race, privilege, and historical capitalism.

"Oklahoma" offers no final opinions. Rather, the poem is a delicate field of inferences and relations. The speaker is neither arbiter, victim, nor soliloquizing hero, but only, as the poem says, trying to arrive at his "midpoint." That is, he is trying to arrive at neutral buoyancy, a state that bears a resemblance to negative capability—what Keats described as "when a person is capable of being in uncertainties, mysteries, doubts, without any irritable reaching after fact & reason." Poised amidst, and surrounded by, such ghostly forces as those represented in the poem, isn't his insomnia understandable?

Caveat about New Forms

This essay does not intend to glorify asymmetry and disjunctness for their own sake. Or to claim, as some do, that artistic techniques of randomness and shuffling construct a better or truer portrait of the world. There is something wrong, perhaps even adolescent, about the celebration of disorder as an artistic principle or virtue. Such sport is a kind of aesthetic drunkenness. I once watched a speaker shuffle the index cards on which his lecture was written, then read them in the resulting random sequence. He had a point to make about order, but there's a "let's shock the bourgeoisie" flavor to such claims and performances, which usually seems like modernist preening. The avant-garde correlation of any kind of organization with an oppressive rationality is false, anyway. And the celebration of randomness, from a certain perspective, seems like playing video games while Rome burns.

Speaking for myself, I don't want to be disoriented except for a worthy cause. I've experienced plenty of disorder in my life, and labored hard to achieve basic equilibrium in my inner and outer worlds. I love art that undertakes the work of framing experience. Orientation, to me, is a pearl of great price. To make even a small amount of sense, to represent the world in a coherent, resonant manner that is not reductive, seems to me a great athletic achievement.

Rigorous Intuition

Maybe the composite structure offers some formal tools with which to address and depict the era in which we live—a strategy that infiltrates worldly knowledge with the individual field of sentience. Perhaps the factual and the subjective can use each other as insurance policies—or as outriggers, to prevent from capsizing into their respective seas. But, the question arises, what are the principles of composite organization? Can the apprentice poet simply throw a lot of unlike yet interesting things together, and voilà, produce a poem? Without conventions of prosody or dramatic structure to organize the shape of the poem, what is the difference between the peculiar orchestration of a good composite poem and the haphazard assemblage of a magpie's nest?

It's a good question without an easy answer, because the key to the making of composite forms lies in the terrain just beyond rationality. The skills that go into the composite poem are rooted in highly cultivated instincts. Even so, a composite field of inferences still has some structure that makes it apprehensible, comprehensive, ambitious, and resonant with the ground of experience.

Two of the skills that seem to be commonly employed in the best composite poems are *layering* and *metaphor*. Layering describes a way of mixing scale, type, and tone, which is parallel, not integrative. Layering is a technique that can capture the mosaic nature of experience that can't necessarily be accommodated in the typical dramatic poem. The layered poem (as embodied in earlier examples of this essay) might include a weather report, a two-dollar hot dog for lunch, a reference to history, existentialist musing, and an incidental conversation.

Part of the reason Tranströmer is such a significant artist is the mosaic nature of his style—eclectic not just in information but in tone and scale as well. He has a consummate ability to suspend and aggregate different systems and realms, for example, the psychological and the spiritual. More specifically, part of his very modern resonance is the way his poems are inflected at one moment by a vacuum-like existentialism, and at another moment by a respectful aftertaste of Christianity. This collusion between faith and disbelief imbues his poems with a distinct atmosphere of values. Between these two positions, which barely rub against each other, we find a contemporary ground that poetry has not previously offered.

Here are two brief samples from Tranströmer's "Baltics," a long composite poem anchored to the landscape of the Baltic Sea, where the poet's grandfather worked as a ship's pilot:

IV
From the lee side,
close-ups.
Bladderwrack. In the clear water, the seaweed-forests shine,
    they're young, you want to emigrate there, lie stretched out
    on your reflection
and sink to a certain depth—the seaweed that holds itself up with
air bubbles, the way we hold ourselves up with ideas.

V
July 30th. The bay has become eccentric—today jellyfish are
    swarming for the first time in years, they pump themselves
    calmly and gently
forward, they belong to the same shipping company: AURELIA,
they drift like flowers after a sea burial, if you take them out of
the water the entire form disappears, like when an unspeakable
truth is lifted up out of the silence and expressed as lifeless gel,
yes, they're untranslatable, they must stay in their own element.

August 2nd. Something wants to be said but the words don't agree.
Something that can't be spoken.

Trans. Patty Crane

Layering of very distinct tones is quietly everywhere here. The speaker, moved by the beauty of the seaweed forests, exclaims, "you want to emigrate there," which comes across as an impulsive emotional exuberance. Slightly later in the same sentence, a detached and much more adult mode of conceptual commentary manifests: "holding itself up with air bladders, as we hold ourselves up with ideas." This layering of ecstatic and analytical selves may not be conspicuous, but it quietly communicates a complex, composite version of internal experience.

Another intellectual gesture, or layer, commonly found in many of Tranströmer's poems is the motif of reiterated skepticism toward language and human intellect. Repeatedly, the inadequacy of words and the limited capacity of human consciousness to meet experience are emphasized; repeatedly the intellect is represented as something unwilling, something employed to hold experience at arm's length. Contrarily, even at its best, the deepest understandings are as Tranströmer says, "Something that can't be spoken." Real truths, we are told—real ideas—are "untranslatable": they explode, die, or become shapeless when they are brought into the atmosphere of ordinary human commerce.

Though Tranströmer's poems are full of such reservations—delivered in a sometimes despairing, sometimes witty tone—the intellect is wonderfully active in his poems. And, although Tranströmer constantly expresses doubt about the reliability of words, he paradoxically uses them with figurative abandon. "I love that cabbage butterfly," he says in "Streets in Shanghai," "as if it were a fluttering corner of truth itself!"

The image brings us to consider the rich systems of metaphor that infiltrate Tranströmer's composite poems. In the excerpts from IV and V of "Baltics," one can see the trope of natural *buoyancy* (first of seaweed, then of jellyfish) being extrapolated in two different conceptual directions. First the seaweed bladders are compared to the human employment of "ideas" as flotation devices (the speaker's implicit judgment upon this human practice is hard to discern). Next we encounter the descriptive buoyancy of the beautiful jellyfish; their fragility, we are told, is like that of "unspeakable truth," which loses all its shape and life when "lifted up" into the common air. The intricate implications of such correlatives between the natural, the textual, and the conceptual are never fully teased out or resolved in "Baltics"; rather, they hover and resonate in the structure of Tranströmer's narratives and thought.

The point worth emphasizing here is that these two metaphors are *not* reiterations of the same idea, of a mind pounding a trope like a piano chord. They are quite distinct uses of similar images drawn from nature—yet the way they cross lines and entangle in the mind is representative of the potential complexities of metaphor, and of how metaphor is used in the composite structure. Like the imagination, like the mind, and like experience, the composite poem reiterates the limits of the knowable, and also the protean, rich connectedness of it.

An equally distinct tutorial in metaphor can be drawn from Tranströmer's droll characterization of the jellyfish: "they belong to the same shipping company: AURELIA." (*Aurelia* is the genus name for one tribe of jellyfish.) On the surface, the comparison between a genus and a corporation is beautifully witty—yet the analogy between organic life and a commercial realm also works in a profoundly integrative way, to "naturalize" and connect the human and organic dimensions of the world.

Such suggestive cross-fertilizations of imagination—both of connectedness and of limitation, of blockages and gaps—are aspects of the composite poem that I admire and love. These instances from Tranströmer's practice demonstrate that good composite thinking is by no means *sloppy* or haphazard; rather, it possesses a subtlety and metaphysical precision that surpasses most examples of poetic discursiveness.

A few of the practicing poets to whom I would assign this label of composite poem makers are Tomas Tranströmer, Campbell McGrath, Robert Hass, Anne Carson, and Fanny Howe. Other, somewhat experimental writers, like Lyn Hejinian, sometimes use the composite poetic structure. So-called lyrical essayists like John D'Agata also structure their work along these modular lines. Poems written in the

Persian and Urdu form called the ghazal often seem composite in their design; their spiritual intention is to inspire associative thinking without resorting to too much closure or didacticism.

The Quixotic Quest of Form

This essay is not intended to be a declaration of the Coming Reign of the Composite Poem. The idea that there is some historical aesthetic march of "progress" in literary forms is silly. A contemporary poem can as brilliantly succeed in a narrative mode, a confessional mode, or as a villanelle describing water lilies, with power and delight. Poems and poets get to select the ground of their endeavor, and, according to their nature, they are as likely to succeed in one as in the other. The idea that every poet has to accommodate the pressures of modernity is alarmingly naive, and constantly disproved by good poems of every ilk surfacing every day.

Nonetheless, as artists, we are seekers, seekers of technical discovery as well as of vision. Every writer I know dreams of a state of perfect fluency and freedom of expression. And thus we are never really indifferent about the possibility of new poetic structural forms, because we are always on a quest for greater expressive power. Endlessly we dream of a sentence structure or voice or stanza that will perfectly accommodate and enable our consciousness. Perhaps we should know better, but we keep on looking, thinking, and listening, hunting that one poet, that singular book, theory, perception, or tonality that will unlock and liberate us.

The anxiety beneath such restlessness is justified, because our personal artistic means are ever growing stale with habit and redundancy; our poems are always falling behind our changing sensibility. Every once in a while we wake up and discover that we are writing poems several steps, or a year or five years, out of date. What we don't know *now*, what the structure of experience is like *now* for us, obligates us to find a new way of saying what cannot be articulated by the old means, in the old vocabulary. Where we are, if we are paying attention, is always on the edge of the unarticulated, in the terrain of the new life.

This is true not just in terms of its experiential particulars—the IV bag, the grown children texting, the neighbor with Tourette's who shouts, "You must change your life"—but also in terms of structure and form. We seek new techniques, and new ways of using old techniques, because we wish to do justice to reality, and we wish to find out how to say more. We wish to stay awake, and art is our chosen instrument for the attempt. It is only right that we keep looking.

Vertigo, Recognition,
and Passionate Worldliness

> There's no solution, that much
> we knew, there are only fragments, and the fact that
> we spoke in complete sentences seemed to us
> a strange joke.
>
> —ADAM ZAGAJEWSKI, "LIGHTNING"

Here are two well-known descriptions of what poetry is and does: one by Wordsworth, one by Stevens:

1. "All good poetry is the spontaneous overflow of powerful emotion . . . recollected in tranquillity."
2. "The poem must resist the intelligence / Almost successfully."

These two assertions, though not opposed, place distinctly different emphases on the function of poetry. The first description, Wordsworth's, suggests that poetry is in part a stabilizing force, a means of gaining perspective on primary experience: powerful emotions can be gathered, then dynamically relived, measured, and digested in the controlled laboratory of the poem. By proxy, such a poem also may guide a reader through the processes of feeling, and offer a tutorial in constructing perspective.

In contrast, Stevens's description implies that the poem and the reader engage in a sort of struggle with each other—that struggle is how they become intimate, how they really "know" each other. Stevens suggests that a good poem, as part of its process, resists, twists, and en-meshes the reader (and perhaps the poet as well), an engagement in which perspective is challenged, and by no means guaranteed.

These two descriptions, of course, are not mutually exclusive, nor exhaustive, on the subject of what poetry does. Even so, the two orientations emphasize two distinct value systems of poetry in a way that seems relevant to our contemporary poetic moment. Two different kinds of poetic pleasure/meaning: Perspective versus Entanglement; the thrill of recognition versus the thrill of disorientation.

What do we, as readers, want from a poem? On the one hand, plenty of poetry readers are alive and well who want to experience a kind of clarification; to feel and see deeply into the world that they inhabit, to make or read poetry that "helps you to live," that characterizes and clarifies human nature. To scoff at this motivation for poetry, because it is unsophisticated or because it seems sentimental—well, you might as well scoff at oxygen.

Similarly, to dismiss the poetry of "disarrangement," of poetry that aims to disrupt or rearrange consciousness—to dismiss poems that attract by their *resistance,* thus drawing the reader into a condition of not entirely understanding—such a dismissal also seems to foreclose some powerful dimensions of poetry as an alternate language, a language expressive of certain things otherwise unreachable. Perhaps language as experiment has ends that are otherwise unforeseeable.

In our time, this bifurcation of motives among poets has become so pronounced as to be tribal. The polarization in premises has been further enhanced by a whole generation of poets who have been intellectually initiated into critical perspectives on language and meaning that render all forms of "recognition art" suspect, problematic—or, even worse, boring. Because the fit between the human mind, the actual world, and language is imperfect, is fraught with distortion, to manifest those distortions in poems has come to constitute a subject matter, even an idiomatic universe of its own, accompanied by a host of lyrical conventions and manners.

The poetry of perspective is well known in its essentials: it is an integral part of the history of rational humanism. This more recent poetry of "resistance," the poetry of de-rangement, has been less clearly described and understood. For all of its theoretical apparatus, we seem still to lack an accessible common vocabulary for the poetry of difficulty, with its feints, rhetorical postures, incompletions, and camouflages. What are its motives, its values, its techniques, and its options? To examine examples of its current manifestations is important for its own sake, and should enlarge our understanding of poetry itself.

First, though, to give *us* some perspective, let us consider an anthem of perspective poetry from the mid-twentieth century. George Oppen's "The Building of the Skyscraper," written in 1965, is a poem in the perspective mode. Though abstract, Oppen writes in a famously plain style, and furnishes his statements with concrete examples. His poem is keenly attuned, in very contemporary ways, to the predicaments of modern dizziness.

> The steelworker on the girder
> Learned not to look down, and does his work
> And there are words we have learned
> Not to look at
> Not to look for substance
> Below them. But we are on the verge
> Of vertigo.
>
> There are words that mean nothing
> But there is something to mean.
> Not a declaration, which is truth
> But a thing.
> Which is. It is the business of the poet
> "To suffer the things of the world
> And to speak them and himself out."
>
> O, the tree, growing from the sidewalk—
> It has a little life, sprouting
> Little green buds

Into the culture of the streets.
We look back
Three hundred years and see bare land.
And suffer vertigo.

Oppen's austere, forceful poem is a beautiful summary of the existential conditions of the twentieth century. One feels the vertigo of dizzy technologic height, of "civilization," of accelerated change and profoundly transmuted circumstances. We have learned, says Oppen's speaker, to endure a great deal of speech that means little or nothing. We learn to screen out certain facts of the environment. We cling with intensity to our immediate situation, the historical present, because not to cling is to fall. But there is, nonetheless, Oppen asserts, something that persists, and our example is the little life of a tree, growing on a sidewalk, into the "culture" of the street.

Oppen performs the role of tribal father in this poem, summarizing our collective situation and placing emphases upon what he sees as crucial recognitions. So this plainspoken, plaintive, yet ambitious poem offers us a point of view and a place to stand, a context within which we might comprehend our feelings relative to our circumstances. Oppen offers no solutions, but the reassurance of a lucid diagnosis. The receptive reader might feel the gratitude of a sick person in a doctor's office upon hearing that her condition has a name. The speaker acknowledges the utility of our coping strategies—that we manage life by blocking much out. And he also places into perspective the responsibility of the poet not to avoid or deflect. On a metaphysical level, the speaker asserts that something exists and persists beneath language, like bedrock beneath the skyscrapers.

It seems important to note that "The Building of the Skyscraper" does not wax nostalgic for the past, nor does it exactly reject the actuality of the present. Oppen's speaker is reportorial; he describes the precarious situation of the soul surrounded by the rapidity and degree of modern change. His is a metaphysics of compassionate realism.

It is the *confidence* of "The Building of the Skyscraper" that may be most striking, even enviable to a contemporary reader. That confidence illustrates how much the art of poetry has changed since 1965. First, the speaker is confident about his authority to speak; he goes at his subject head-on. Second, the speaker is confident about the capacity of language to point with subtlety and discrimination, even when being implicit.

With contemporary poetry in mind, one could say that the *what* in Oppen's poem has remained the same: we are deep in the storm of modernity, without shelter or map. The *how*, however, has changed: the how of poetry's response. Judging from current magazines and books, vertigo—"a sensation of whirling and loss of balance, associated particularly with looking down from a great height; giddiness"—is the preeminent topic of contemporary poetry. It may be the dominant stylistic inclination, as well. In the context of our time and place, this artistic focus—of speed and rapid, or no, transition—makes perfect sense. After all, our economic culture specializes in two things: surfeit and counterfeit. The lack of relative scale between the component parts of our existence, the swamp of excess information in which we each day swim, and our paradoxical lack of influence on that world—they make us ill. We have data sickness. Add to that our drastically increased sense of the corruption of commercial and political speech, and of the instability of language. Surely our resulting collective dizziness is a fundamental symptom of modern life, one to which poems naturally refer.

But, like "I love you," there are so many ways to say vertigo. A thousand kinds of vertiginous poetry are currently being written, from Ashbery to Zapruder. Vertigo can be dramatized, ventriloquized, celebrated, satirized, goofily lamented, or critiqued in poems. One poem might be a cry of claustrophobic distress; another might rejoice in the whirlwind of modern phenomena; a third might be intent on exposing the epistemological instability of language; a fourth engages in a mode of lyrical thinking whose terms never become quite clear. And—here's the rub—the surfaces of those poems may look very similar. Though easy enough to mimic—"the poem must resist the intelligence"—

vertigo is a slippery project to handle in a dramatically effective way. "Almost successfully."

Now is a good moment to say, straight out, *intention matters.* Intention is a kind of attention, and the underlying attention of a poem (not necessarily singular, not necessarily preordained) is the agency that has discovered and calibrated its effects. When we read a disorienting poem, we ask ourselves, "what is the expressive premise for which this vertigo is an idiom?" By way of illustration, it might be said that the contemporary practitioners of poetic vertigo can be temperamentally divided into two camps: negative or positive. One zone of poetics is planted in the ground of what Lyn Hejinian calls "antagonism to closed structures." The other group is aimed at the discovery and celebration of "imperfect meanings." The difference is not to be detected in the often-similar poetic surfaces but in the *spirit* of the poems.

The most prevalent poetic representation of contemporary experience is the mimesis of disorientation by non sequitur. In this mode the poem issues a series of disparate statements, impressions, dictions, and tones without defining the relations among them. The poem of nonparallelism—how things and words coexist without connecting—is the "red wheelbarrow" of Now.

Here's a standard example of the mode, the beginning of "Elective Surgery," by Lewis Warsh—declarative, nontransitioned, and irregular, an attention-deficit poem:

> You think you can begin as if it were ten years ago & you were
>   still that person
>
> A woman turns her head to catch a glimpse of her former lover
>
> I offer you the key to a city without words
>
> The guy on trial for rape wears glasses to make him look studious
>
> The policeman arrested a soldier for fondling a single parent

> Sometimes I create an imaginary aisle in my mind: we're
>   walking down it,
>   arm in arm, into the sunlight outside the church
>
> The woman who approached my car & asked for a light wasn't a
>   prostitute
>
> You can escape your responsibilities by going to the movies or
>   getting drunk

Warsh's poetic mode, of which this is representative, might be described as soft-core disassociation, gathering sticks and bundling them together in a kind of rickety mismatched bouquet. The common underlying tenor is impossible to discern. Depending on a reader's aesthetic sympathies, the disorientation of such a poem might be appealing or repulsively dissonant.

A critic operating from the perspective camp will fault this poem for being diffuse, indulgent, blurry, and so on. "Elective Surgery" overflows, but it aims for no Wordsworthian integrative vision from its tranquillity. Because the frame insistently slides around, neither a narrative nor a thematic picture comes into focus.

A reader of the "resistant" persuasion might find the poem charming in its dodgy ambling, its refusal to settle into one field of vision. You could say that Warsh, in a modestly postmodern way, *evades* focus, thus embodying a contemporary disorientation. Although "Elective Surgery" doesn't create much dramatic tension, or direction, it possesses an idiosyncratic energy that comes from the streetwise tone and the unpredictable zigs and zags of the sequence. The poem's personality disorder has personality. Warsh's poetic mode embodies a contemporary manner of poetic pleasure whose wobbling pivot engages and resists the intelligence of the reader.

In the work of some poets, the poetics of non sequitur are employed less amiably. Ben Lerner's collection *Angle of Yaw* clearly intends to represent the modern environment—the maelstrom of 24-7 information and the omnipresence of media manipulation. The poems themselves aim to work upon us corrosively, tearing up our internal information systems as much as any hacker. Like Warsh, Lerner also uses non sequitur as a primary technique:

> THE AIRCRAFT ROTATES about its longitudinal axis, shifting the equinoxes slowly west. Our system of measure is anchored by the apparent daily motion of stars that no longer exist. When the reader comes to, the writer hits him again. Just in case God isn't dead, our astronauts carry sidearms. This is not your captain speaking, thinks the captain. A magnetic field reversal turns our fire friendly. Fleeing populations leave their bread unleavened, their lines unbroken.

"The Aircraft Rotates" creates disequilibrium by constantly jumping its track, using declarative non sequitur assertions to disrupt continuity and disorient the reader. Its speed and its use of ventriloquized, dislocated but familiar speech samples invoke the surfeit of information in modern life, the impersonal, bossy, and hip bureaucratic chill of speech, and the uncertainty, in this maelstrom, of locating any fixed perspective. All is relative: much knowledge is received and unreliable; there is no captain, and even language itself, like the term *friendly fire*, is duplicitous. It is a rhetorically disastrous landscape, in which all the old paradigms are awry. And our narrator? Clever and knowing, but not friendly. "When the reader comes to, the writer hits him again." In their way, Lerner's poems represent a state of trauma, a world of too-muchness, where nothing connects.

Lerner is a poet of political inclinations, but not a believer in rational method, nor in the persuasive manner of intimate conversation. Rather, his poems seem anarchistic and Dionysian—they manifest the centrifugal whirlwind of modernity from inside. One might say that the speaker is channeling the collective psychosis, splicing and dicing a slew of rhetorics. The most striking and "resistant" thing about "The Aircraft Rotates" may be its enigmatic point of view. The omniscient narrator speaks from an undisclosed position, in a tone hard to "read": is it bitter, amused, helpless, sarcastic? In its manner, Lerner's poems fit the description of "Elliptical" poets offered by critic Stephen Burt: "they admire disjunction and confrontation . . . are always hinting, punning, or swerving away from a never-quite-unfolded backstory; they are easier to process in parts than in wholes. They believe provisionally in identities . . . but they suspect the I's they invoke." Elliptical or not, "The Aircraft Rotates" denies the reader clear purchase for innerness; the declarative rhetoric of the poem creates a carapace of attitude. And, since sentences arrive in such fierce non sequitur rapidity, we don't know if the speaker is *reporting* this frothy modern thrashing of comprehension, or *administering* it, like some savage jester. Such is the enigmatic stance of Lerner's poems. Such poems intentionally offer no harbor for the traveler, neither consolation nor explanation. It's a prosody of, and about, violence. The instinct of the demolitionist is strong here. Here's another poem from *Angle of Yaw*:

A WALL IS TORN DOWN to expand the room and we grow distant. At the reception, cookies left over from the intervention. In the era before the flood, you could speak in the second person. Now the sky-lighted forecourt is filled with plainsclothesmen. I would like to draw your attention. Like a pistol? In the sense of a sketch? Both, she said, emphasizing nothing, if not emphasis. Squint, and the room dissolves into manageable triangles. Close your eyes completely and it reappears.

Lerner is clever, worldly, and resourceful, but his poetic mode of quick changes tends to come off as ironic or antagonistic. His topic isn't just the untrustworthiness of perception and perspective itself, but the wild duplicity of our era. Plainclothesmen, a flood, an intervention: it's not *event* or *narrative* here that is missing, but the lack of any centralizing emphasis that makes reading the poem maze-like, hollow, and circular. It is a poetry both confrontational and evasive. Lerner's relentless focus on the contextless "angle" and "yaw" of contemporary consciousness is a representative preoccupation of his generation. If the Plath generation was obsessed with psychological extremity, if the

1980s generation was obsessed with narratives of self, the generation of the aughts has been obsessed with exposing the fallibilities of perspective. But what comes after?

Rusty Morrison's "please advise stop" poems (there are sixty-four in her book *The true keeps calm biding its story*) also practice the stylistics of vertigo. Each poem is a semifragmentary, declarative sequence of phrases, set against a murky but discernibly oppressive narrative background. Unlike Lerner's poems, Morrison's overall tone is not knowledgeable irony but wary pathos; this narrator is a pilgrim in a strange world, a vulnerable if never-identified speaker:

> **please advise stop**
> walked barefoot in the spill of loamy earth between redwoods
>   stop
> accompanied by no sermon stop
> my repetitive gesture will eventually wear through its surrounding
>   world please
>
> I heard a drawer pull open but not its philosophies rearing up in
>   jagged peaks stop
> how to walk off the hackles we raise so carelessly stop
> how does a sequence continue to startle its way through clouds
>   of conclusions please
>
> wash one's face of any resemblances before they mingle stop
> I don't see color in the window at moonrise but feel it a dampness
>   on my forehead stop
> tattooed both wrists with the holy idea but only skin deep please
>   advise

Implicitly, the halting disjointedness stands for the psychological disruption of an individual inner life. Yet it seems the speaker's traumatized state of being is not psychological (this isn't an abuse narrative) but a metaphysical sense of endangerment. Thus, though emotionally plaintive, Morrison's poems include plenty of intriguing conceptual assertions on the subject of cognition itself. Morrison and Lerner share the obsessive subject matter—"how do we know?"—but are different in emotional register: the one aggressive and socially satirical; the other bereft and distinctly private. But, like Lerner, Morrison combines a forceful thrusting prosody with a disjunctive form to represent a system in extreme disorder.

Morrison's poems combine sophisticated self-consciousness with stylistic primitivity—one of contemporary poetry's most appealing hybrid combinations, as in the work of C. D. Wright, Jorie Graham, and D. A. Powell. At its best, this makes for a potent representation of interior vertigo. In fact, Morrison's fluttering, anxious prosody resembles Graham's darting graphs of consciousness.

For all their disarticulation, Morrison's poems employ an elaborate formal fiction. "please advise stop" is one of sixty-four poems with the same title and three-tercet form. The end words of every three-line stanza are the same: *please, stop, please advise*—words meant to evoke not just the speaker's emotional condition but the clipped grammatical format in which Western Union telegrams were once sent.

The framing conceit of this compressed referential form is richly suggestive: a nameless traveler in a far-off land, in distress, is reporting back, and asks for advice through a narrow technological aperture (the telegraph sentence). Vertigo is thus both the story and the style of these poems. By issuing each line as a broken-off, truncated unit, shunning continuity and complex grammatical relations, the poems imply a world where things do not accrue sense nor progress as story. It is a choppy, chopped-up world, at best, and a chopped-up speaker, as well. The lack of capitalization and punctuation likewise keeps us adrift, implying a landscape of no boundaries:

> the road to the asylum forks each time I genuflect please
> the entire morning gone callow with a rationale stop
> now even the least leaf rustling must be theatricalized please advise

The poems in *the true keeps calm biding its story* are full of velocity, keenly phrased, and conceptually acute. There are scores of intriguing, aphoristic lines to savor, like the ones quoted here. The conceptual self-consciousness of lines like these alert us to the epistemological dimension of the speaker's crisis. Many lines in "please advise stop" explicitly emphasize the futility—and in a weird way, the falsehood—of making experience cohere. The content of any one moment does not—perhaps *must* not—connect to any other in the past or future: "wash one's face of any resemblances before they mingle." Thus, the speaker is exiled in manifold ways: physically, religiously, and hermeneutically. This world is post–Humpty Dumpty: the speaker cannot put it together again.

To their credit, Morrison's poems are not *emotionally* obscure—they wear their existential poignancy on their sleeve. With an appealing frailty, this traveler's voice is self-conscious yet vulnerable, a representation of the anxiety of the contemporary soul/self. In manner and matter, this is a poetry of ardent trauma.

Here's another poem from Morrison's series:

> I add brush-strokes to my visions to thicken their surface
>   courage stop
> novelty prodding me with its impatience-stick stop
> my flashlight held high under the blanket stop
>
> we can't let the actual contain us the same way every time stop
> the sound of a rolling boil is satisfying and frightening stop
> it's the past that's finishing every sentence for me please
>
> between the sigh and the laugh was it a genuine repair or a
>   quick dab of polish stop
> the low ceiling was uncoiling at the exact speed I recoiled from
>   it stop
> grant the visible its pronouns and watch it disappear please advise

The true keeps calm biding its story contains abundant virtuosity, and talent to burn. Nonetheless, after reading nine or ten "please advise stops," one begins to feel exhausted. It takes a lot of work to stay tuned to a present that steadily deconstructs itself, that refuses to make a history. And no discourse does accumulate, because in this universe, each moment, each insight, each breath, each memory is transient, anonymous, and oblique; each insight reiterates its instability. The reader waits in vain for something besides the speaker's disconcertedness to manifest—more "plot" of some kind. "We can't let the actual contain us the same way every time," the poet says, in heroic resistance to phenomonological complacency. But the sequence itself suffers from exactly this flaw, a kind of homogeneity of disruptedness. The instability of this world eventually registers as a feverish and telegrammatic numbness. Samuel Beckett made great literature of such modern spiritual deprivation, and he too used repetition as a device. Yet sixty-four episodes of "please advise stop" require us to ask: Can we praise a book for its intriguing concept, and method, or even its brilliant individual lines, if the method creates monotony?

Of course, this is an issue, not much acknowledged, that haunts much experimental poetry: the use of disrupted poetic forms results in a *style* but resists *shape*. Thus individual poems very often lack individual dramatic identity. Such poems may be remarkable and ingenious in their process, but they are almost impossible to remember. Shapelessness is a hazard of the poetics of vertigo, and of the non sequitur style. How this affects their value as art is hard to say. Is memorability no longer a primary aesthetic criterion?

One might extrapolate, from these several examples, the features of a period style—a love for the rhetoric of authoritative declaration, coupled with a love of disjunction, peppered by reflexive observations about the act of composition, remarks about cognition and textuality. Here are the characteristics of the period style I observe:

1. A heavy reliance on authoritative declaration
2. A love of the fragmentary, the interrupted, the choppy rhythm
3. An overall preference for the conceptual over the corporeal, the sensual, the emotional, the narrative, the discursive

4. A talent for aphorism

5. Asides that articulate the poem's own aesthetic procedures, premises, and ideas

I don't know if I've got this list right; surely I am omitting some features. But it is curious how much contemporary poetry bears some combination of these stylistic features, even when the poets are concerned with quite different possibilities of poetry. Morrison and Lerner are certainly very different, and both are marvelously talented writers. And yet there is a kind of pitching-machine assault in their prosody, a buffeting of dizzy richness. Is this assertiveness of quantity and momentum a kind of correction for the general helplessness of our circumstances? Is it reflective of a new aesthetics of "confrontation," which strives to overwhelm with velocity and facility? One question we can usefully ask in regard to a particular style or poem is, what is the range of feeling, or sensibility in this poetry? Is it narrow, or deep, or various, or broad? Is it merely whimsical, merely disjunct, merely antagonistic, or can it also be friendly, entertaining, and spacious?

One American poet who has been trafficking in disorientation for a long time is James Tate. Tate has passed through a dozen phases in his career to date, but is probably most frequently labeled as a bonnie prince of whimsical American surrealism. His work of late has been in prose poems, in which his picaresque speaker and characters are spinning through life, inquisitive and clueless as Candide, trying to identify and accommodate the fiction of whatever world they are living in. Here is the opening of "The Rules":

> Jack told me to never reveal my true identity. "I would never do that," I said. "Always wear at least a partial disguise," he said. "Of course," I said. "And try to blend in with the crowd," he said. "Naturally," I said. "And never fall in love," he said. "Far too dangerous," I said. "Never raise your voice," he said. "Understood," I said. "Never run," he said. "I wouldn't dream of it," I said. "Never make a glutton of yourself," he said. "It won't happen," I said. "Always be

polite," he said. "That's me, polite, " I said. "Don't sing in public," he said. "You have my promise," I said. "Don't touch strangers," he said. "That's forbidden," I said. "Never speed," he said. "You can count on me," I said.

Here is a vertigo that accumulates. Tate's poem relishes the comedy of absurdity, but its tale also becomes progressively more dreadful as it goes on. In the past, Tate's subject matter has been the illogic and haplessness of private psychic life. But in *The Ghost Soldiers,* his narratives suddenly seem social and political—more about our collective disorientation and estrangement as citizens than about the eccentricity of an individual speaker. In "The Rules," the universe seems to be a bizarre police state; the subject of the poem becomes the innumerable unspoken rules that bind us, our tragic willingness to cooperate, and the consequent foreclosure of wonder.

In Tate's effectiveness an argument is to be made for the poetic power of context. His narrative frame may be slight, but it offers the reader a place to stand, and the opportunity for identification. When we read a poem like "The Rules," we see modern vertigo rendered in manners as absurd and forceful as those of "The Aircraft Rotates" or "please advise stop," but more directly and more movingly. These vertiginous poems share much in subject matter, but they have very different timbres.

As "the rules" are enumerated, one after another, we are able to relish the shifts in implication between, for example, the command to "Never ride on a blimp" (absurd) and "Don't touch strangers" (poignant). Tate's poem of disconnectedness provokes pity, recognition, and laughter. Here is the end of his dizzy two-page long poem:

"No sushi," he said. "Oh no," I said. "No fandango," he said. "Not possible," I said. "No farm bureau," he said. "Not my style," I said. "Beware of hypnotism," he said. "Always alert," I said. "Watch out for leeches," he said. "A danger not forgotten," I said. "Stay off gondolas," he said. "Instinctively," I said. "Never trust a fortune-teller," he said. "Never," I said. "Avoid crusades," he said. "Certainly," I said.

"Never ride on a blimp," he said. "Blimps are out," I said. "Do not chase turkeys," he said. "I will not," I said. "Do not put your hand in the mouth of a horse," he said. "Out of the question," I said. "Never believe in miracles," he said. "I won't," I said.

This conclusion feels heartfelt, deflating, and true, in part because it has been formally prepared for. As a longtime reader of Tate, I feel that his genius has reinvented itself once again, this time as an allegorist and satirist, an American Kafka. ("The Rules" is a cartoon version of "The Trial.") *The Ghost Soldiers* is a fat book, containing nearly one hundred poems, not all of them political. But Tate's picaresque imagination has an unerring knowledge of, and tenderness for, human fallibility; at the same time his recognitions about the pathos of modern life, as borne by idiom, manners, and tone, are pitch-perfect. In the mode of fantasist parable, there's no better representation than these poems of what it is to be in the middle of America now. Psychological eccentricity is no longer the topic of Tate's narrative melodies, but collective tragedy. Here's another one:

Desperate Talk

I asked Jasper if he had any ideas about the coming revolution. "I didn't know there was a revolution coming," he said. "Well, people are pretty disgusted. There might be," I said. "I wish you wouldn't just make things up. You're always trying to fool with me," he said. "There are soldiers everywhere. It's hard to tell which side they're on," I said. "They're against us. Everyone's against us. Isn't that what you believe?" he said. "Not everyone. There are a few misguided stragglers who still believe in something or other," I said. "Well, that gives me heart," he said. "Never give up the faith," I said. "Who said I ever had any?" he said. "Shame on you, Jasper. It's important to believe in the cause," I said. "The cause of you digging us deeper into a hole?" he said. "No, the cause of people standing together for their rights, freedom and all," I said. "Well, that's long gone. We have no rights," he said. We fell silent for the next few minutes. I was staring out the window at a rabbit in the yard. Finally, I said, "I was just

saying all that to amuse you." "So was I," he said. "Do you believe
in God?" I said. "God's in prison," he said. "What'd he do?" I said.
"Everything," he said.

What is more tragic, and in this case, less true, than the speaker's
disclaimer: "I was just saying all that to amuse you"? At the end of
"Desperate Talk," we feel the absurdity and pathos of human ignorance, and the echoing vacancy of the social landscape. Even so, we
are able to breathe inside Tate's poem, and to sense the development
of sympathies, shades, and transformations because, for all the errancy
of text, we are given the gift of context. With the asset of that third
dimension, a narrative frame, the poem makes room for the reader,
and gives us a chance not just to be bewildered but to respond.

Lyn Hejinian, present at the birth of the LANGUAGE movement,
is one of the most venerable experimentalists writing, and still one
of the freshest. Inventive and discursive, omnidirectional, nonlinear,
her best work has a humane quirkiness. Alternately dipping into the
textual and the experiential, sometimes straightforward and sometimes wildly errant, her work doesn't want for speculative intelligence
of many kinds. But in Hejinian's writing, one feels the attachment of
the speaker. Though she is dead set against predictability, her method
doesn't feel like a lunge for novelty, or an obedience to an ethic of deconstruction, but like a comfortable, well-worn style of dress. As a
consequence, in a Hejinian poem, ideas are shaded and fleshed by experience, and vice versa. Her work is simply more three-dimensional
than most poems, conventional or experimental:

> It is January 7 or perhaps it's a thank you note. "Our moods do
>   not believe
> in each other," as Emerson says. Instead
> of creating realities art gives us illusions
> of illusions—so says Plato and for Plato
> little could be worse. Would you agree
> with Plato? B wants to liberate phrases

from the structural confines and coercive syntax of sentences
   and so
does C but C is in France. A sense of the uniqueness
and interrelatedness of things is fundamental here. It would be
   hard to
          go farther
than a mile from home for groceries and the fun of it
without noticing the canyon's rosy mouth
which is very like the one in Zane Grey's randy landscape.

Hejinian deals in the same contemporary verities as the other poets considered here—unknowability and transience, the illusory nature of selfhood, the limits and instabilities of language—and, like them, she is deliberately irregular in her progressions. But Hejinian handles her material in a quasi-discursive, quasi-autobiographical manner, comforting for its intimacy and intermittent physicality. "B wants to liberate phrases / from the structural confines and coercive syntax of sentences and so / does C but C is in France": it's the worldly acknowledgment of that last *but*—"but C is *in* France"—that makes Hejinian lovably worldly.

The relationship of the vertiginous to *flatness* in poetry makes an interesting sidebar: LANGUAGE poets like Clark Coolidge and Charles Bernstein have sometimes insisted on the flatness of text as a purist principle, a kind of ascetic prohibition of illusion. Hejinian's *The Fatalist,* though intentionally disjunctive, is nonetheless stubbornly three-dimensional. With her pedigree in deconstruction, Hejinian naturally accounts for language as material, and fractures the rules of predictability in syntax and sentence. Yet in her dippy, erratic mapping of the human condition, all concepts are not created equal. This poet does not balk at sincerely asserting some hierarchies: "A sense of the uniqueness / and interrelatedness of things" she says, "is fundamental here." The passages of *The Fatalist* are weighted with various dimensions and tones: the sensuous gratifications of nature, the history of other persons' sayings. The effect is to keep us on our toes and, at the same time, to keep us company. At times I feel that Hejinian, in her generous claims about the spaciousness of human nature, has become the unlikely humanitarian of her tribe:

> Time is filled with beginners. You are right. Now
> each of them is working on something
> and it matters. The large increments of life must not go by
> unrecognized. That's why my mother's own mother-in-law
> was often bawdy. "MEATBALLS!" she would shout
> superbly anticipating site-specific specificity in the future
> of poetry.
> . . . . . .
>
>   Materiality, after all, is about being
> a geologist or biologist, bread dough rising
> while four boys on skateboards attempt to fly.

Hejinian practices a method she calls "free concentration," which tracks the changing presence of consciousness like rings sliding past on the surface of a river. Elements of randomness and deconstruction are part of the flow, as well as passages of considerable continuity. Thus *The Fatalist,* as a non-begining-middle-end kind of project, is not notable for its dramatic arc. It is written in episode-like paragraphs, which might be described as the journal entries of a playful intellectual. Whimsical, intermittently serious, the density changes and, admittedly, might be hard to stay with in a cumulative way. The observation recurs: an experimental poet, almost by principle, chooses improvisation over cumulative dramatic shape.

I suppose that may be part of *The Fatalist's* message—process, not product. Pulling it all together is not the point, no more than pulling it all apart. But even though we may not be "getting anywhere," Hejinian rewards us with the company of a rich, generous, and experienced sensibility. As a reader I feel the united, collaborative commitment of intellect and feeling, idea and material, the author's ongoing, affectionate meditation about consciousness and its connection to human life. As a result, there are plenty of passages in *The Fatalist* that make me happier in the reading—partly *because of* their diffidence—than most other recent poetry. Maybe this *is* esoteric stuff, poetry for the initiated, full of loose ends. But *The Fatalist* also teaches one how to read it. One of its pleasures is the adventure of syntax; Hejinian believes in having fun with the sentence, not just making war on—or with—it:

> Feeling the slowness of the wide world fleetingly I'll speak
> to the points that make me hesitant to be
> enthusiastic constantly but bearing in mind that translators
>   *often* say
> obvious things smugly
> sure that they know what their audience doesn't, namely another
>   language
> that has let them in on a secret—and it is so often *French*!
> The deadline for "dialogue" comes and is gone.

Another pleasure of Hejinian's vertigo is the constant change of pace; there are eddies and resting places, alternations in color, mood, and, may I say, "landscape" that embed the poetry in the human milieu. Hejinian, like other poets discussed here, is declarative and frequently disjunctive; she doesn't want the reader to be complacent, but even so, one doesn't feel baited or battered or shown off to. Hejinian's intention is to be a singer-thinker, to implement a way of writing not confined to one plane of reference. One feels in *The Fatalist* the fluency of a lifetime of thinking and practice, and a dexterity in improvisation that doesn't have to be forced or rehearsed any longer. Hejinian's poetry achieves an imaginative balance between the poetry of perspective and the poetry of disorientation, and honors the role of both in human life. Perhaps even more important is the way that Hejinian has learned to use her technique not to map, or recount, in the Wordsworthian sense but to exemplify the spaciousness of the world—verbal, conceptual, perceptual.

None of the poets discussed here is Wordsworthian, recollecting in tranquillity, restoring order to the dizzy modern condition. None attempts to establish the tranquillity of a justified mind. Yet in the words of Oppen's "The Building of the Skyscraper," Hejinian knows that "there is something to mean." She studiously doesn't want to box it in or to "conclude" it; neither does she generate great additional anxiety that the sky is falling. "It is the business of the poet," writes Oppen, "to suffer the things of the world and to speak them and himself out." In its passionate, compassionate worldliness, *The Fatalist* offers the presence of a reassuring adult, who has been around the non-Newtonian block. Even if we are falling, we can feel that we have some human companionship in the descent and that we are having an adventure.

"Regard the Twists of the Bugle / That Yield One Clear Clarion": The Dean Young Effect

Dean Young is the contemporary avatar of avant-garde populism in American poetry. His poems are jazzy, imagistic, ironic, romantic, humorous, surrealist-inflected, and accessible. They gratify the expectations of art and of entertainment. Without dumbing down for his audience, his allegiances to pop culture, his anti-intellectual asides, and his slangy Americanski patter serve to hold his poems in the gravity field of the general reader. Though influences are certainly visible in Young's work (New York School poetry, French surrealism, John Ashbery, etc.), he has refined and honed a poetic mode and texture distinctly his own. Young's own aesthetic influence among young poets is widespread, and though he is not the only model for the style du jour, his work brings into focus certain values and habits of our poetry era—speed, dissociation, parody, romantic irony.

What's amazing in the standard Dean Young poem is how much quickness, vocal inflection, and data are packed propulsively into each cubic foot, as in this opening of "Learning to Live with Bliss":

> Kissing a rose is a dumb thing to do
> not just from the rose's point of view.
> But it's a start
> like driving off a cliff's probably a finish.
> In between you'll want to go to Mexico,
> get so drunk you think what you're doing is a dance.
> Remember though, tattoo removal is costly, painful
> and depending on your insurance

they might use a sharpened stone.
Wondrous is the matter of this temporary world.
Regard the twists of the bugle
that yield one clear clarion.
Regard the neuron's long run
from spine to pinkie's tip.

The world described in Young's poems is an unstable and, in fact, violent place, always changing texture or ripping itself apart, unraveling and reassembling into beautiful and horrible shapes. Against the instability of this universe, we have a narrator of great rhetorical alertness, veering between ecstasy and anxiety. The elastic comedy and intellectual resourcefulness of this speaker serve to camouflage the dread and tragedy of the cosmology, narrating through zigzags and smashups, through bad news and good. The texture is so recognizable as to be an aesthetic signature: fast, daffy, tragic, witty, vivid, fabricated by the paradoxical collaboration of associative and disassociative powers—interrupted at times by epithets of wisdom and grace.

A second feature worth remarking on in this representative passage is that, for all the activity of the voice, it is discursively clear. "Learning to Live with Bliss" is an argument in favor of the pursuit of beauty, a hazardous (driving off cliffs), absurd (dancing in public), but worthwhile (wondrous) quest. One hazard of an improvisatory style is disintegration—a poetics of continuous generation is always threatening to lose, or to get tangled up in, its own thread. In a Young poem, we get plenty of surprising twists and turns. But it is perhaps even more surprising to notice the coherence of so many poems. In fact, examined closely, Young can start to look like quite the discursive poet. "Learning to Live with Bliss" concludes with images that figuratively signify the endlessly teetery balance between completion and incompletion, creation and destruction, knowing and ignorance, which is a central credo of the worthwhile life:

... who doesn't like tipping stuff over?
See those tots stacking blocks

> just so they can knock them down?
> They're in training.
> They're working up to kissing a rose.

In a Young poem, the thematic core often vanishes in a kind of dust storm, then reappears. It is this reappearance of theme within the poem that distinguishes him from a steadfastly ambient poet like Ashbery.

The essential earnestness in Young's poetry can be easily overlooked in the razzle-dazzle of the surface. Constant mobility for him paradoxically serves to keep a sort of gyroscopic balance. "Learning to Live with Bliss" displays a characteristic pattern of development: opening proposition, dexterous comic development, vernacular self-deprecation, and then a surprising shift into a less colloquial, more formal and dignified expressiveness—here, of wonder: "Wondrous is the matter of this temporary world." The drunken wiseguy banter turns out to be a Sufi dance. The inverted grammar of the line not only connotes formality but also pushes the poem toward several elevated meanings—both senses of "matter," as in *material* and *theme*. The theme is wonder; the matter is wonderful.

It's that ambidextrous affluence of idea and image, that Cirque du Soleil facility of acrobatic performance, that have made Dean Young one of the most widely published, admired, and influential presences in the landscape of American poetry right now. Put simply, his poems make it seem like their writer is having a lot of *fun;* these performances also offer an enticing, enviable appearance of freedom. Young has published ten-plus books in the past twenty years (that's roughly five hundred poems in the books alone), won numerous prizes—Guggenheim, NEA, and so on—and has been featured in *Best American Poetry* anthologies almost continuously. He publishes with equal frequency in the *Paris Review, Fence,* and the *Believer,* and is as well known to a younger set of readers and writers as Mary Oliver or Billy Collins is to the NPR crowd.

Even more than those poets, Young's mode has been adopted and adapted, replicated, mimicked, and multiplied by hordes of young

(especially young male) poets. Any teacher-poet who has read manu-
scripts for competitions, or screened applicants for prizes or graduate
program admissions of the past ten years, can recognize, like a tattoo
or a piercing, the stigmata of the Dean Young devotee: the breathless
velocity, the wisecracking asides, the spiraling out and in, the disjointedness of development, the Crackerjacks quality of the imagery, which
combines beauty, smart-aleckness, irony, vulnerability, and kookiness.
There are legions of little Dean Youngs out there, advancing on the
capital like pirates with dilated eyeballs and blue hair.

Young appeals to, and serves, at least two camps of readers, the
theoretical crowd and the hotdog–baseball fans poetry crowd. He has
enough theoretical fluency, enough metatextual reference, to be accred-
ited as a postmodernist on the one hand, and enough regular-guyness to
appeal to the poetry reader in the street. He can sound like Billy Collins
in one moment, or like Robert Hass or John Ashbery in the next.

Here, for example, is Young in the vernacular, regular-guy style,
flavored with idiom and domestic Americana detail; though the poem
zigs and zags a bit, the speaker is intimate:

> You're not going to like this,
> says the mechanic. Fine.
> I already don't like people sending me
> pictures of their children not because
> I don't appreciate wee Marta eating paint chips
> or Alexander thrashing his horsie
> but how does one dispose of such photos
> without weird mojo?
> ("Don't Need a New One, Just Fix What You Got")

In an Ashberian mode, such as that of "I Can Hardly Be Considered
a Reliable Witness," the occasion of the poem is (like Ashbery's own
work) self-generated, self-generative, and opaque:

> First there was a raffle conducted by silhouettes
> then some gaga clangor and the deflection

of not getting what I wanted probably never.
I was trying to write The Indomitability
of the Human Spirit to impress you but
it kept coming out The Undomesticated
Human Spigot, a blowhard stoned soap opera.
I couldn't understand anything and you
were my teacher. The rain bounced off
the upturned canoes by the man-made lake
and out of the man-made water small bodies
propelled themselves into the nevertheless air.

This I could not do.

I had been worn out by a lasagna
A train had run through my almanac.

In contrast to such abstract expressionist self-sufficiency ("I don't even *need* a topic"), a poem like "Colophon" features a much more traditional poetic undertaking, a theme no less traditional than an ode to autumn, sensuous, ripe, and dying. It's this naturalistic Keatsian lyric mode that might be most surprising to Young's casual readers:

More than the beetles turned russet,
sunset, dragging their shields, more than
the crickets who think it's evening all afternoon,
it's the bees I love this time of year.

Sated, maybe drunk, who've lapped at the hips
of too many flowers for one summer but
still must go on hunting, one secret
closing, another ensuing, picking

lock after lock, rapping the glass,
getting stuck in a puddle of dish soap,
almost winter, almost dark, reading far past

the last paragraph into the back blank page,

. . . .

I don't think there's any way

to prepare.

The steady, unviolated tone in "Colophon," the passionate yet elegiac sound, and the sensuality of the language all identify Young as a bona fide and gifted Romantic poet. "Colophon" is straightforwardly an ode, a lament not just for the speaker's personal mortality but for the mortal everything. For all the kiltered manners, Young can be poetically effective in perfectly traditional, even sumptuous, ways.

Some True Things about Dean Young's Poems

Young is often described as a surrealist poet, but that label is somewhat misleading. Surrealism is a twentieth-century form of radical romanticism, yes, but Young's romanticism is more old-fashioned than that. The priority of theme in the work has already been mentioned, and Young's persistent themes are textbook (big R) Romantic ones. He has a well-formulated worldview that testifies to the supreme force of the individual imagination, the opposition of the individual to mass society, the divinity of nature compared to the malfeasance of humanity, and, especially, the tension between the transcendence of the ecstatic moment and the corrosive nature of horizontal time. As the poem "Colophon" shows, Young is closer to Keats than to Breton.

What Young's poetics do have in common with surrealism is their commitment to the poem as event, that is, textual improvisation as proof of life. The unpredictability of such a poem, inventing itself on the spot, is essential to its authenticity. What such poems must prove, beyond whatever their incidental "subject" might be, is the invincible vitality of the human imagination. The imagination is always the true hero of such a poem. In this sense, a surrealist poem is never allowed to descend into sorrow or nostalgia, as a romantic poem might; for a surrealist, states of rest are stagnancy. Vitality is essential, whether it is a mode of violent contortion, as practiced by Breton or Tzara, or romantically soaring, like Éluard.

Another way in which surrealism is relevant to Young's poetics is in the frequent function of Eros as creative source: the imaginary beloved (always a woman) symbolizes mesmerizing mystery that summons the poet in her fantastic pursuit. The negligee is the cape of the muse; the boudoir is the chamber of mystery. Eros in the surrealist economy is not mere horniness but the opening of the primal channel that runs from the unconscious to the fantastically pursued future. The poet is a channel for cosmic Eros. The ecstatic stream of the poem in process is a self-fulfilling romantic fugue. Despite their historical connection with Freud, surrealists are not psychologists, working through neuroses, but devotees—poetry is their art of wooing the divine. The following section from Young's "Ready-Made Bouquet" showcases the metamorphic tangos between improvisation and the theme of romantic love:

> . . . Loving someone who does not
> love you may lead to writing impenetrable poems
> and/or staying awake until dawn, drawn to airy
> azure rituals of space ships and birds.
> Some despairs may be relieved by other despairs
>
> as in not knowing how to pay for psychoanalysis,
> as in wrecking your car, as in this poem. Please
> pass me another quart of kerosene. A cygnet
> is a baby swan. Hatrack, cheese cake, mold.
> The despair of wading through a river at night
>
> towards a cruel lover is powerfully evoked
> in Chekov's story "Agafya." The heart seems
> designed for despair especially if you study
> embryology while being in love with your lab

partner who lets you kiss her under the charts
of organelles but doesn't respond yet

later you think she didn't not respond either
which fills you with idiotic hope very like
despair just as a cloud can be very like
a cannon, the way it starts out as a simple
tube then ties itself into a knot. The heart,
I mean.

As rapidly shuffled and pasted-together as these materials seem, they are also persistent in their coherence. One way to describe Young's work might be "turbulent"; another might be "spiky." Like a sea urchin or a porcupine, its quills bristle out, both entertaining and warning us not to come too close to the violence of creation. To call this a kind of defense mechanism is accurate, but it also offers the disarming seduction of disheveledness. Leaving things out, restoring them, Young swerves between irony and wonder, between coherence and incoherence, always (well, usually) giving wonder the edge.

The American modifications to the imported surrealist aesthetic (which have turned surrealism from a theology into a fashion statement) have been two, both visible here: ironic tonal deflation and a certain kind of cartooniness in the use of image. American surrealism (consider the poets Mark Strand, James Tate, and Thomas Lux) usually has a kind of auxiliary self-conscious goofiness, an acknowledgment of the difference between the literary reality of France in 1915 and of twentieth-century American culture. Young's poetic incorporates these American features but retains the essentially heroic mission of surrealism proper. Though one steady theme of Young's poetry is human limitation and folly, as a poet he is nonetheless afraid of neither strong feeling nor ideological grandeur. Like Kenneth Koch, the member of the New York School poets with whom he has most in common, Young is at bottom an ecstatic. He doesn't concede to powerlessness. In Young's poetry—unlike that of most of his imitators—the striving nearly always breaks through to transcendence.

The Followers

We are living in a time of poetic explosion; the university creative writing systems have not just trained a lot of young poets in literary craft, they also have fermented these young artists in a broth of language theory, critical vocabulary, and aesthetic tribalism, which the age apparently demands. The New Poetry, called by some "ellipticism," can be generally characterized as stylistically high-spirited and technically intensive, intellectually interested in various forms of gamesmanship, in craft and "procedure," acutely aware of poetry as language "system." These young and not-so-young poets have learned many techniques for disassembly, deflection, ventriloquism, miming, theatricality, misdirection, and feinting. The Self, in their manifold species of poems, is more theatrical than confessional or meditative. As a result, their notion of poetic voice is not so much voice as an organic extension of self but voice as an artifice, a fabrication of vocabularies and rhetorics. Such a poetic voice proves itself by constant and erratic motion, throwing off guises one after another.

Consider the beginning of a poem by the young poet Glenn Shaheen. Shaheen's poetry capitalizes on the colloquial and idiosyncratic, angular voice, flavored with a mild stand-up comic surrealism:

> There wasn't a spot open on the nuclear submarine, so I became
> a seventh grade teacher. I knew
> I needed to stop mixing my fantasies
> with reality. For some social reason
> or other. At a party,
>
> I refused to drink any of the green beer. My rhythm
> took hold of me. I danced
> in front of many strangers. Some of them threw coins. Others
> propositioned me for sex. Some were even
> attractive women. A logger
>
> cuts through a redwood he is strapped to, but then realizes
> he is strapped to the falling part. . . . There wasn't

a spot open in the local fire brigade, so I criticized
the media's saturation of the word *hero*. In another world

I could have been mayor.

> ("In the Spirit of Forgiveness, I Present Heartbreak
> Delegation with a Bushel of Florida Oranges")

A young poet could do worse than this style. It begins with a Woody Allen self-deprecating two-step that counterposes romantic versus unromantic destinies. The narrative that follows has a buoyancy of imagination, dexterity, and a serious undertheme—the competition between the reality principle and the pleasures of fantasy. As in many poems by Young himself, perplexedness is a central stance of this style: the charming, picaresque speaker who staggers through the world, mucking up his own enterprises, while also making discoveries about human life. There's even a pleasing, vulnerable Holden Caulfield mournfulness under Shaheen's duck dance. Then there's the abrupt non sequitur, a metaphorical jump in field of reference: "A logger / cuts through a redwood he is strapped to . . ." This is an apparent jump cut, but one that idiosyncratically attaches to the theme of haplessness.

Yet there is a downside, as well as an upside, to imitation. To begin with, Young's admirers have a difficult act to follow. It is a bitter fact of life that the neural associative capacity of a Dean Young is pretty rare. His method suits no one as well as Dean Young. The nets of association whose spaces he adroitly negotiates, others fall through. The transformative associative cornucopia that tumbles out of his poems by the bushelful seems, not the result of will, but of a born and cultivated genius. Elliptical as they might be in presentation, Young's poems have the intrinsic strength of arising from a unified psyche.

The energetic hijinks of Young's style to some extent can be simulated, but the coherent underdiscourse is less easy to emulate. Young's more facile imitators achieve a texture that is manic, energized by zigzag and ellipsis, but ultimately many of these poems turn out to be more intellectually incomplete or passive than their models. The professions of mystification in Young's own poems are countered by breakthroughs of vision, recovered from or converted into testimonies of romantic compensation. But his poetic nephews and nieces often manage only to portray a speaker who is entertainingly baffled and dismayed. They are able to break up but unable to put together.

Likewise, Young's poems, as a consequence of their deep integration, sustain a state of vulnerability and openness that anchors their ironic transmogrifications and jokester antics. It's this passionate sincerity that is ultimately impossible to "fabricate," because it goes beyond aesthetics.

Subscribers to the Young aesthetic appear in many versions, and, when less successful, embody distinct types of limitation: one type can seem hysterically hyperactive; another hidden inside a shell of theatricality. Others can seem enmeshed in postures of relentless irony. Other poets mistake the disassociative for the associative; thus their poems take obliquity itself for the end of poetry.

"Pastiche with Occasional Botany and Art," by Michael Loughran, offers an example of postmodernized American surrealism without a keel. A zany quasi-associative sequence of image and assertion, the poem creates a lively surface texture of comically disparate images, authoritative diction shifts, and the impression of sense making. Yet it ends up being a sort of kooky whirligig, dependent on the charity of the reader's serotonin. Here is the entire poem:

> When humans avoid low temperatures
> love exists,
>
> which accounts for Miro's
> *Flame in Space and Nude Woman:*
>
> it resembles a car ingesting a raindrop
> version of itself. In good health, corn plants
>
> can transpire two quarts of water
> in a day, whereas the succulents traffic

water to their fleshy parts
through wide root networks,

hoarding it there, sportingly. Conversely,
bamboo commits suicide every 33 to 66 years.

"Nowadays," said Miro at 67,
"I rarely start a picture from a hallucination."

Melvin Calvin discovered one single organ
can perform a large number of functions:

the human heart is known to migrate swiftly
and without warning, like a glove tossed from

the height of a tall statue.

"Pastiche" keeps the reader off balance with its askew sequence of
gestures but to no real end. Aside from a hinted-at topic of love, the
poem possesses no center; it creates no coherent thinking or feeling;
thus it builds no internal pressure; thus it achieves no meaningful clo-
sure. It throws boomerangs that never come back. With its interesting
mixture of materials, and its structure of implied analogy, it promises
relations but doesn't deliver; therefore, it remains cryptic and silly.
Louise Glück, in her essay on ellipsis, says that as a poem of omission
progresses, the content of the unsaid should become increasingly loud
and more precise. Unfortunately, that doesn't occur here. The poem
ends up standing, and falling, on the slim crutch of image, gesture,
and absurdism. The poem is theatrical yet indeterminate. Thus even
its tone is hard to read—indecisively frozen between straightforward
and ironic.

"Charcoal and Ochre Constructions on a Bone Black Ground,"
by Jeff Baker—only a section of which can be quoted here—likewise
displays a voice, manners, and tactics that might be seen as borrowed

from the New Poetry zeitgeist: it presents the polyvocal, alternately daft/grave rhetoric of a young poet. Baker's poem has muscle: the tone is heroic and the language is plentiful and confident. But the poem on some level seems torn between its identity as a poem of robust feeling, and its identity as theatrical production of language:

> Meet me in the basement of the abandoned
> schoolhouse in Cosgrove.
> Feel your way around the wall
> until you find the furnace.
> I will be standing in the coal chute.
> Don't say *windflap* unless you're ready to make love.
> This painting
> is drinking from the skull of its enemy, has lost its people, has lost
> its mind.
> This painting has no flowers left to burn, but like moonshine
> its blooms inside your chest.
> Rose of heat.
> When one died, elders
> stirred hematite with seal fat and put the body red into its grave.
> Then,
> I rose like living blood into the afterlife.
> The player piano of this painting
> sits between mouse-colored curtains in a ghost theater.
> Its arrangement
> of excisions is spread upon the stage like a skin.
> Take this fibula,
> these hooves, take these antlers or tusks.
> Shave what you can into a clay
> vessel and cover.

This is rich writing in tone and image, and its jump-cutting simulation of speed is energetically attractive—but its love for channel surfing sabotages it as art. The chanting element, the narrative element, the comic element—each potentially interesting in itself—have no coherence together. The poem employs some of the passion and furious imagery of the surrealistic lineage, but it can't forgo pop irony ("Don't say *windflap* unless you're ready to make love"). Does it want to be self-referential ("This painting . . . This painting")? Or to be prophetic ("I rose like living blood into the afterlife") in tone? Here we have a lot of verbal imagination, but the poem is so busy changing rhetorical outfits that nothing accrues.

To put it differently, there's a way in which its consciousness of itself as a "construct" leaves "Charcoal Impressions" caught between poetic identities: between poem as visionary rant and/or a postmodern replica of that sort of poem. Thus, like a Civil War reenactment, its authenticity is inconsistent. Baker's style suggests that he might be well suited to be a robust and passionate poet; but, infected by the stylistic hyperactivity of the moment, the poem squirms ironically underneath its own substance. For all the potential richness of "hybridity," such splicings can be a dysfunction as easily as a function. The acquisition of speech gestures is part of every writer's apprenticeship, but not to be able to attach those gestures effectively or excitingly to one's own psychic necessity is to remain only a technician, not a poet.

Poetic values don't just wax and wane, they rotate and splinter and invert. To read much recent poetry is to realize how undervalued *quiet* (different from minimalism) is right now and, conversely, how attractive obliquity and hyperactivity have become as poetic values. But constant motion in a poem provides no resting place for emotional fullness. Ironically, the epidemic proliferation of the New York School voice, itself humanist in spirit, has been another contributing agent to the New Poetic whimsy. The decibels of whimsy have been turned up, the decibels of humanism down. Most profoundly, in their emphasis on style and subversive forms, in the enshrinement of idiosyncracy, too few of the New Poems aspire to the most ambitious mission of poetry, namely, to enlarge our sense of the world: of possibility and human nature, of thought and feeling.

Back to Young

It is hardly fair to employ Dean Young's work, so worth celebrating in itself, as a straw man to characterize an aesthetic sea change. Nor to fault the older poet for the enthusiasm of his cult. Young's poems, even in their dervish whirl, manage to sustain both flight and gravity, simultaneous contact with irony and vulnerability. Like all aesthetic achievements, this richness is both a matter of technical savvy and character, and it is thus especially hard to imitate. Yet a few specific features of Young's work are well worth singling out. One is his allegiance to worldly particularity, which is integral to his dialectical virtuosity. Here, in the opening images of "Vintage," one can see how perceptual fidelity furnishes the materials for the jazzy figurative thinking that is essential to Young's poetic. Because the poem's images are drawn not from pure fancy or verbal ingenuity but from the familiar world, multiple tones can be convincingly evoked without seeming merely theatrical:

> Because I will die soon, I fall asleep
> during the lecture on the ongoing
> emergency. Because they will die soon
> the young couple has another baby.
> She's not out yet but it's late enough
> to see her struggle like a dancer
> in a big bubble. Because the puppy
> will die soon, he learns not to pee
> on the carpet.

Relative to the productions of many of Young's own poems, this passage may look pretty domesticated, but it gives us the chance to consider some of the secrets of Young's orchestrations. If we look at these three case studies of "because we will die soon," we can see the conceptual counterpoint embedded in the figures. Each vignette features a different response to fatality: the first (falling asleep) is ironic, the second (reproduction) is romantic, the third (house-training) is comic-tragic. The interplay between these vignettes displays how Young characteristically uses collation, coordination, and contradiction to achieve a dialectical tension and inclusiveness.

Apollinaire (who was *not* a surrealist) invented the term *simultaneism* for a poetic visionary mode that tries to testify to everything happening at once. Simultaneism is a proposition intimately relevant to Young's poetic—which, like Apollinaire's, is a poetics of ecstasy. Young's poems contain all kinds of gaps, discontinuities, and illogical swerves. They change attitudes like a manic-depressive comedian, but they are not dissociative; they are complex organic medleys that suspend multiple tones and suggestions in a zone of simultaneous coexistence. In that sense, to identify Young's poetic strength with "voice" may not be as accurate as to describe them as charged, self-modulating fields of signs. This presentation of simultaneous multiple realities can be seen again in the conclusion of "Vintage":

> ... Impeccably
> the insects groom themselves, each foreleg
> ending with what looks like a mascara brush.
> Your eyes go on being the sky's,
> beautiful sentiments set off to oblivion,
> while across town the new opera's booed.
> You walk among the racks of dresses absently
> clattering the hangers. So many blues.

Simultaneism is important because Young insists that it is *all* true. The baby in the bubble of the mother's stomach, the serrated legs of insects as mascara brushes, the doomed puppy, the unpopular new opera; the cosmic sentiment that "your eyes go on being the sky's." The manifold, debased, self-canceling, and reproductive world humbles us with its simultaneity. "Vintage" begins in blasé irony, turns toward paradox, then tenderness, and finally arrives at reverence.

Young's body of work is a surprising hybrid of romantic and modern instincts. It celebrates errancy, misunderstanding, and mistaken identity, but makes clear that such mistakenness exists in continuity with nature; the poem is at once a representation of life, an analogue for it, and an independent creative event. Like a good postmodern poet, Young frequently reminds the reader of the textual nature of the poem, of the artifice of poeticized emotion; of the deceptions, shortfalls, and instability of language, and the freestanding independence of art from obligation. Nonetheless, the poems insist too on their naturalness, their commitment to matters of life as much as to signs.

In these polyphonic streams of data, irony is a frequent guest star, but so, also, indefinably, is affection for the world, and an insistence on the truth and value of beauty. The poet's stance is sometimes one of hip distance, but alternately one of openness and vulnerability. In Young's poems, the self is not a theatrical prop, but the representative human soul who aspires, stumbles, suffers. "Of course it's ironic and absurd," he says in a recent commentary, "but that is perhaps only the first lurch, the lurch against habituated sincerity that must happen to gain or at least approach, as corny as this sounds, an emotive truth. . . . Whammo. Irony can't be gone around, it can only be gone through."

In a recent poem, "Non-Apologia," Young makes fierce and playful arguments about not excluding any aspect of poetry, because to do so amounts to an exclusion of life. "Non-Apologia" is the sort of poem in which Young shows his terrific ability to swiftly shift poetic weight between discourse, image, sound, and meaning, all tumbling over each other. Hiding and revealing are sides of each other, doubt makes the vulnerability of irony evident, the word is the poster child of the thing. "Non-Apologia," in a classical rhetorical ploy, begins by proposing the superficiality of modern poetry, then turns to defending its glory and relevance:

> Maybe poetry is all just artifice,
> devices, hoax, *blood* only there
> to rhyme with *mud,* signs wandering off
> from that picnic blanket where once
> the word lounged with the naked girl
> of meaning for Manet to paint. Now
> we think we're not mistaking

the escaped squid for the cloud of ink
but the squid keeps coming back
in its miraculous mood-alterable skin
just as words never stop escaping back
into meaning, word *electric,* word
cardiovascular, falling short, sure,
word *derriere* falling short of the actual
ass you'd lief fondle instead
of reading and writing about squid.
Don't we love words too for themselves,
how *liquid* is almost *squid*
but worry about *laughter* in *slaughter?*
It's always one way *and* the other.
Poetry paints nothing but it splashes
color, flushed, swooning, echolocating
and often associated with flight
. . . .

Even spiders sing. We are all arpeggios
make that archipelagoes but oh, the butter
of your utterance unbanishing me
from the island of myself.

"Words never stop escaping back into meaning" is a fair rebuttal of the absolutist postmodern position that all signs are only signs. But then again, the poet often says, they slip back into being only words. What comes through in the "miraculous mood-alterable skin" of "Non-Apologia," as in most of Young's poems, is their passionate conviction that everything matters intensely, most especially the freedom of play. Indifference and dismissal are never more than brief positions in a graph of possible credible positions, set in testy relation against commitment and affirmation.

The many young writers and readers who are electrified by the poems of Dean Young, and who decide to take up residence on the lawn of his aesthetic, don't just do so for the jazzy riffing or the entertainment. In an era of hip zaniness and dislocation, they are drawn to a sense of conviction inside Young's buzzing poems, to an emotional testimony that includes wonder and the heroic assertion that life and experience are cosmic and participatory. Those writers are not wrong in seeking stylistically what they love in substance; but ultimately they will have to locate their own terms of poetic identity, just as they find their identities in the world outside poetry.

"I Do This, I Do That": The Strange Legacy of New York School Poetics

What a wild history the New York School of poetry has had. When it appeared in the 1950s, it seemed to be a minor art league, a post-collegiate avant-garde boys' club, and a sort of witty, urbane, campy friend to serious poetry—lots of talent and fun, but not much gravitas, and no "orchestral" power. Uninterested in making major statements, the New York School was a style in part conceived around the principle of unself-importance, and that is how it was often perceived, as well—as unpretentious, charming, and light.

In the midseventies, as an undergraduate at the University of Iowa, I don't remember any of my workshop teachers mentioning O'Hara. The standard initiatory diet was Robert Lowell, Berryman, Bishop, Kinnell, Rich, Stafford, Wright, John Logan. Plath was made much of, of course. The last Pound scholars (every English department once had one) were still in operation; some had a sideline concession in Charles Olson studies. Ashbery had not yet gained ascendance. Ed Folsom was teaching Gary Snyder in the literature class down the hall. Sherman Paul was teaching Robert Duncan. Even to a veteran aesthetic eye in the landscape-shifting sixties and seventies, it must have looked like the New York School was and always would be over-shadowed by the Beats, the Confessionals, and even the Projective Verse clan.

Twenty years later, in, say, 1995, the landscape had transformed profoundly. The highly wrought style of midcentury modernism, which had truly begun to decline in the sixties, was by then in full reces-sion; the plain style had ascended (and then commenced to decline).

W. C. Williams had long since displaced Eliot as a sponsoring pater-nal force. In Buffalo and San Francisco, smart people were sitting at LANGUAGE poetry readings, their faces locked in a rictus of atten-tiveness. Add fifteen more years, to bring us to the present, and Robert Lowell, the most monumental poet of his era, is now much less influ-ential than his "frivolous" contemporary, O'Hara.

As of our present moment, the New York School of poetry, like the alluvial fan at the mouth of a river, has broadened and stretched out into multiple strands of influence, including shoals of post-Language "compositionalist" work, playful surrealism, urban walking-around poetry, campy literary "Personism," mildly disassociative party po-etry, post-Beat, and so on. Ashbery's influence on American poetry may turn out to have been, in its way, as large and irreversible as that of Auden or Eliot in their times. But even more than Ashbery, Frank O'Hara has had the most widespread, infiltrating impact on the style and voice of American poetry in the past thirty years.

The true achievement of the New York School was to invent and bequeath a humanist avant-garde to the American tradition. O'Hara's tones and rhythms, his styles of mobility, have become tid-ally influential, especially among youngish poets. Sociability, asso-ciative speed, a love of perceptual and social detail, the affectation of scatterbrainedness, an intimate voice of self-deprecation and badi-nage, dazzling offhand abstract asides, and more, they all stem from O'Hara. In the affect and spirit of that era, magazines like *Jubilat, Conduit, Fence,* and *Forklift, Ohio,* and presses like Wave, Verse, and many others seem very much an echo and continuance of the high-spirited independent mode of the mimeographic sixties Manhattan scene. One could even argue that the brave, goofy freedom of the Talking Heads comes from the New York School. It's not possible to map or count the tentacles and tribes of the New York School academy.

Yet, influence is a funny thing; like DDT, or Prozac, these sub-stances get into the water supply, and you don't know where or how they are going to turn up again. And here's the bad news: the aesthetic traits of O'Hara passed down to us have not been universally beneficial in their absorption. One of the less healthy has been a poetical style of distractedness. Another is the manner of hapless self-unimportance.

Berrigan and the Second-Generation New York School

Some of this, history suggests, can be laid at the unassuming feet of the second generation of the New York School, which altered and diffused the legacy. Influence gets passed, not just *from,* but *through,* generation to generation, and it metamorphoses in the passage. The energetic legacy that came from the first-generation New York School passed into a succeeding era of antipoetics, the intentionally disheveled poetics of Ted Berrigan and company, whose zeitgeist brought poetic unpretentiousness to a new height.

By virtue of his presence, dedication, and charisma, Berrigan is generally conceived to be the odd successor to O'Hara's genius for community building, following O'Hara's death in 1965. Berrigan, a great admirer of O'Hara's, was the avuncular center of the St. Mark's Poetry Project, which flourished in the late sixties and seventies, a scene that included Tom Clark, Dick Gallup, Tony Towle, Alice Notley, Anne Waldman, Lewis Warsh, David Shapiro, Peter Schjeldahl, and dozens of others. Many of these poets went on to different, often notable destinies, but there was a period when their experiments with I-do-this-I-do-that aesthetics, flavored with a druggy pop surrealism and some Olson-inspired Projective versification, were vivid with the cultural moment in SoHo, the Bowery, and Greenwich Village.

Berrigan himself wrote some beautiful individual poems, and his collection *The Sonnets* is considered a milestone in the poetics of expressive fragment and collage. But most of his aesthetic is built around a style of supreme haplessness. Here, for example, is section 6 of the long poem "Tambourine Days," a work of high unseriousness:

> Now I'm going to read 3 cereal poems:
> CORN FLAKES
> OATMEAL
> RY-KRISP

> thank you
>> they were composed
> excuse me
> I mean NOT composed
>> using the John-Cage-Animal-Cracker
>> Method of Composition
> (this seems to be mushrooming into a
>> major work
>>> of high
>>>> seriousness)

>> I'd fight for that!
>> (I didn't have to.)

Spaced out on the page, distracted, full of domestic minutiae and vagrant parentheticals, dropped lines of thought, and goofy asides, Berrigan's poems, and those of many of his peers, declare their harmlessness with a vengeance. They are ruled by the muse of defiant triviality: Disheveled Lite. To say so is not to illegitimate the art; second-generation New York Schoolers embodied a valid bohemianism, an anti-highbrow, fiercely anti-commodity aesthetics, around which a whole community swirled, publishing mimeo magazines, giving poetry readings, talking art and life. Unpretentiousness, aesthetic and otherwise, is a long-standing American virtue. And it was, in the sixties, an avant-garde for its time. It would have been a glorious time to be a young poet in New York.

Still, something was misplaced in this dogleg turn between the past and future, between one generation and the next. There is, in the work of the first generation of the New York School, an erratic yet recurrent summons to loftiness that rarely appears in the succeeding generations. O'Hara, with his deep knowledge of other arts and his robust genius, brought an improvisational nobility to his work, a warmth, dignity, and humanness, as a few lines from his "Sleeping on the Wing" can remind us:

Fear drops away too, like the cement, and you
are over the Atlantic. Where is Spain? where is
who? The Civil War was fought to free the slaves,
was it? A sudden down-draught reminds you of gravity
and your position in respect to human love. But
here is where the gods are, speculating, bemused.
Once you are helpless, you are free, can you believe
that? Never to waken to the sad struggle of a face?
to travel always over some impersonal vastness,
to be out of, forever, neither in nor for!

Though the passage has gestures of blithe scatterbrainedness, the romantic heroism enacted here is equally real, the struggle of a visionary speaker with the terror of his own freedom: "Once you are helpless, you are free"; "Never to waken to the sad struggle of a face?" Koch and Ashbery, in their distinct ways, also deploy such moments of rhetorical loft, which can be tracked to Emerson, Stevens, Baudelaire. What such grandeurs exhibit is the healthy egotism of a generation that trusted its own authority. For all their youthfulness and joie de vivre, those poets posessed a belief in the seriousnes of Art with a big A, which may have been lost in the twisty-turny aesthetics of our own time.

Contemporary Mannerisms

What *are* some of the disadvantageous gestures and mannerisms that passed from New York School poetics into our present-day atmosphere? First, the coy mannerism of distractedness, often embodied by the device of parataxis (disjunction) and non sequitur. Second, an affect of goofy personal ineptitude that effectively precludes stances of both tragedy and heroism—offering, instead, the charms of melancholy and cluelessness as characteristic poses.

Here, for example, is a stanza from "Thanks and Acknowledgments," published in the magazine *Fence:*

IX
He called his stapler 'Hegel'
They adjusted the margins to accommodate his ego
The chain passed smoothly over the teeth
The text opened into sentences
If this were an actual emergency, it would be more sudden
He pastiched his way to a cult following
They said he had fourteen days to vacate
He'd like to think he beat them to the punch

This goofiness, with its quick-sequenced, non sequitur enactment of clever, addled adolescence, is one embodiment of latter-day New York School poetics. It draws on the streak of absurdism that runs through the tradition. Any reader of much contemporary poetry will recognize the manner—harmless in itself, rather cute, an artistic style that serves a slightly hallucinogenic sherbet for dessert.

So much for distractedness. On a nearby page of the same magazine, a poem called "I saw a theft occur" serves as an example of the more hapless style du jour:

I saw a theft occur.
I had just come through the glass doors.
I had come for my essentials: soap, shampoo, batteries.
The culprit brushed against me and making
even strides across the parking lot
disappeared into a field of tall grass
under the glimmering stars.

A man in uniform ran into me
cursing. Idiot, he said, if you don't get
out of the way I'll blow your brains out.
I saw a theft occur, I said, the culprit brushed against me.
I had just come in, I had come for my essentials.
Tears came then into his eyes.

He peered deep into my soul.
Help us, he said, my building is near
and my partner will make you dinner.
Your building is near, I said, and your partner
will make me dinner. Yes.

The inconsequentiality here is deliberate, an aesthetic joke proffered in the bland-faced tongue-in-cheek mode of the second-generation New York School. The neuteredness of tone and the minutiae of the narrative record are nutty and charming in a way that might be compared to the art of Andy Warhol or Roy Lichtenstein. The speaker's feckless-ness is part of the art as well as part of the story.

The self represented in both these poetic instances is not very deep, it is true, but more significant is the relative *passivity* of the speakers; they are sweet but flattened someones to whom experience *happens*. How can we find any power or subject matter in these poems beyond the personality of speaker? We may dignify these performances by saying they satirize and enact the breakdown of meaning in contemporary society; we can smarten up our appreciation by noting that such text exposes its own textuality—but who really cares, after reading a half-dozen such poems?

Charming Ineptitude and Melancholia

Of the two mannerisms, distractedness and haplessness, the latter is the more dangerous, because of the way it fatally softens and dis-empowers the self of the poet or the speaker. At the same time, hap-lessness lowers the stakes of poetry itself. (One might ask, by way of proof, what major figures have emerged from the second- or third-generation New York School of poetics?) The predominant feeling-tone of such poems is a kind of melancholia that registers the speaker's sensitivity, while also communicating that she or he is powerless. But, we might ask, is the ambience of sensitivity worth the price of passiv-ity? And what are the long-range consequences for us and our poetry?

Nothing is more addictive for a poet, nor, we could say, more definitive than tone. Tone wears on its sleeve, or carries latent in its depths, an entire worldview. To encounter a special literary tone can be as revelatory and empowering as any plot or argument. Yet, to repeat, tones may also be habit forming, and an attachment to one tone may preclude all others.

Ironically, New York School manners are the source of many of the most likable traits in American poetry: an observant unpretentious speaker, alive with mobility, character, and engagement, taking the world personally. Yet too often, passivity seems to come with the contemporary package—the idiom is lively but also feels neutered, frivolousness, or soft. The speaker is vulnerable and perceptive, yet powerless in the world.

Matthew Zapruder is one of the best younger poets now writing, and one of the most talented grandchildren of the New York School legacy. In many ways, his poems incarnate the zigzaggy and melancholic gestures I have been describing. But his book *Come On All You Ghosts* exhibits both the inheritance of the third-generation New York voice and a determined struggle to overcome the self-enclosure of its contemporary practice.

This struggle deepens the resonance of the poems into something more existential and resounding, and conveys implications that remain after the charm has passed away. To illustrate how Zapruder transcends the baseline mode of idiosyncratic charm, and the manner to which he is heir, I want to quote the entire poem "Schwinn" and to call attention to what happens at its conclusion:

> I hate the phrase "inner life." My attic hurts,
> and I'd like to quit the committee
> for naming tornadoes. Do you remember
> how easy and sad it was to be young
> and defined by our bicycles? My first
> was yellow, and though it was no Black
> Phantom or Sting Ray but mutely a Varsity
> I loved the afternoon it was suddenly gone,

chasing its apian flash through the neighborhoods
with my father in vain. Like being a nuclear
family in a television show totally unaffected
by a distant war. Then we returned
to the green living room to watch the No Names
hold our Over the Hill Gang under
the monotoned chromatic defeated Super
Bowl waters. 1973, year of the Black Fly
caught in the Jell-O. Year of the Suffrage Building
on K street NW where a few minor law firms
mingle proudly with the Union of Butchers
and Meat Cutters. A black hand
already visits my father in sleep, moving
up his spine to touch his amygdala. I will
never know a single thing anyone feels,
just how they say it, which is why I am standing
here exactly, covered in shame and lightning,
doing what I'm supposed to do.

It is easy to imagine O'Hara beginning a poem, "I hate the phrase 'inner life.'" The first half of "Schwinn" is the speaker's effort to retreat into the affections and carelessness of American boyhood. Nonetheless, Zapruder's closing turn fiercely challenges the romantic premises of what has preceded—its own dreamy chronicle of affection—and by doing so countermands its own tendency to evade the inner and the outer life as well. That confrontation adds a necessary gravitas and force to the poem:

> . . . I will / never know a single thing anyone feels, / just how they say it, which is why I am standing / here exactly, covered in shame and lightning . . .

Zapruder brings to the page a particular, deep-seated, neurotic, and quite real problem of his generation, one that the first generation of the New York School did not have to deal with so intensely: the

instability or insubstantiality of language, which makes assertion difficult and consequently isolates the artistic self more than ever. The
first-generation New York School writers had a Dada consciousness
of the arbitrariness of language, but their relation to it was on a vol-
untary basis. For the current generation such self-consciousness is
almost an obligation. Thus it's the speaker's self-conscious acknowledgment of the *consequences* of weightlessness and disconnection
that brings the poem "Schwinn" most emphatically into the realm of
poetic substance. It's the acknowledgment of the shortcomings of all
that precedes—the banter and memory and anecdote and wit—that
elicits the *poignancy* of the inadequacy of poetic means in a way that is
especially human and natural.

At this moment in the poem, one witnesses the emergence of the
adult figure that has shadowed the poem all along. If the poem is a
kind of playground of affections, this note at the end of the poem is
the presence of death accepted into the body of the speaker; thus, the
world is suddenly realized. Zapruder's ability to, at pivotal moments,
move into the foreground or forefront of his poems and speak clearly,
with directness and vulnerability, is what distinguishes his poems from
those of most of his peers. He doesn't just practice the weightlessness
and zaniness of the New York School, but he is substantial enough to
delve into the consequences of such a style—consequences that seem
central to our moment, culture, and lives.

I was talking about this New York School stuff to my friend David
Rivard, and he added some relevant thoughts about the relative cultural contexts of then and now. The culture as a whole right now, he
said, superficially resembles the social energy of the New York School
much more than did the culture of the fifties. Our present environment is already speeded up, superficial, bright, distracted, sensation-
filled, and wholly approving of personal pleasure as a birthright. This
puts contemporary poetry in a much different situation than then. The
first generation of New York poets invented themselves *against* a back-
drop of conservative fifties American culture—a context against which
their aesthetics meant something fresh and liberating, even spiritual.
Consequently it might be reasonable to think that what contemporary

culture needs from poetry right now is a counterposition, something with weight and existential gravity, asserting countervalues.

Conclusion

If there's a kind of heroism and commitment missing from contemporary American poetry, that absence is surely born of many forces: middle-class manners, media saturation, a sense of powerlessness as citizens and humans, embarrassment for same, a more insular and self-conscious poetry world than has previously existed. The result is a seeming inability to consider what the culture, local and at large, might require, and to imagine the capacity of poetry to provide it. It is paradoxically true that a lack of felt authority is accompanied by a difficulty in imagining responsibility, the responsibility required for our time, our moment, our humanness. The negative historical narrative about confessionalism is that it shrank the compass of our poetry to a narcissistic focus on the personal, but at least that poetic generation did not stint for conviction and intensity. The hapless, distracted poems of the moment seem to miss the whole issue. Where's the duende and fierceness of mind that authorizes vision in our time?

Freud said that questing for truth was at bottom masochistic, because it means seeking a thing that will cause you pain. He further said that the urge to inflict truth on others is sadistic—a warning for all critics! But not being *able* to find the truth, or feeling *capable* of such a quest, not feeling *qualified* to possess or enunciate it, is another kind of neurotic tragedy. One of the questions of the poetics of our times is, Can the pleasures of mobility, deflection, fragmentation, and wit be joined to the resonance and gravity of adulthood?

The aesthetics of the New York School bequeath a kind of vitality, speed, and élan that still nourishes American poetry; it will never vanish from our national poetic selfhood. Even so, the aesthetics of haplessness and daffiness are a compelling contemporary problem— one that will have to be grappled with in this and future generations.

◇ ◇ ◇ ◇ ◇

Unarrestable:
The Poetic Development
of Sharon Olds

What do you get as a reward for being a poet like Sharon Olds? For having written five-hundred-plus poems that plumb the range of family dynamics and intimate physicality with a precision and metaphorical resourcefulness greater than ever before applied to those subjects? For having permanently extended and transformed the tradition of the domestic poem? For doing as much, single-handedly, to win readers to American poetry, as any poet of the latter twentieth century? For making poetry seem vital and relevant to young and not-so-young adults all over the place?

Well, you win great popularity. You are loved by many, for reasons alternately well founded and misconceived. You are run down by envious peers and overlooked by academics. Your name is invoked like a brand name to denote the obviousness of confessional poetry. You are accused of repetition, narcissism, and exhibitionism.

And you get some very weirdly flavored critical reactions from American literary critics. Here's William Logan, reviewer for the *New Criterion*, discussing *Blood, Tin, Straw*, Olds's sixth collection of poems:

> If you want to know what it's like for Sharon Olds to menstruate, or squeeze her oil-filled pores, or discover her naked father shitting, *Blood, Tin, Straw* will tell you. If you want to know what her sex life is like (it's *wonderful*, trust her!), she'll tell you, and tell you in prurient, anatomical detail the Greek philosophers would have killed for—she's the empirical queen of lovemaking, of every secret session of the body. . . .

She may start a poem complaining about her labia, but, before she's through, her womb is heaven and her husband's French-kissing her god-tongues. (You'd think the god's small tongue would be the clitoris. How lucky of Olds to have more than one.)

. . . Olds may someday become the laureate of the bedroom; but for all her radical pretense (she claims if she hadn't married she'd have been a Weatherman bomber), she's a homely *Redbook* moralist, believing in motherhood, family, and honey on her nipples. By the time she's reduced to giving sex tips, or calling her husband's member "the errless digit," all her shallow pretense is greedily on display.

The kindest thing you could say about this is that it is shockingly ungenerous—but that would be too kind. In fact, Logan's tone is so swollen with spleen, and so obsessive, that its private underpinnings seem obvious. What's additionally disturbing and even embarrassing about this review is the unconcealed fascination of the critic with naming body parts, like a little boy looking through a knothole in a neighbor's fence, touching himself while cursing in Latin. It is criticism flavored with weird jealousy, topped by puritanical disgust and condemnation. Therapy, anyone?

And here are some excerpts from an essay on Olds by Adam Kirsch, a younger critic:

There is a reason why there have been so many poems about love and so few about sex, I mean the act of sex: and these examples demonstrate it. . . . It is only when sex is made to serve as a metaphorical focus for more elaborate and entangled feelings that it rings true, and becomes poetically alive. And since Olds has one simple and finally unsurprising feeling about sex—that its bodily goodness refutes its social or religious badness—the varied descriptions of sex in her poetry are monotonous.

But Kirsch, for starters, may be missing the poet's point: that biology is never just biology either; it is its own legitimate counter-theology. Here is "Prayer," one of the poems Kirsch offers as evidence for the prosecution:

> Let me be faithful to the central meanings:
>
> the waters breaking in the birth-room which suddenly
> smelled like the sea;
>   that first time
> he took his body like a saw to me and
> cut through to my inner sex,
> the blood on his penis and balls and thighs
> sticky as fruit juice;
>   the terrible fear
> as the child's head moves down into the vagina.

It is hard to imagine why these images would seem simpleminded and monotonous to the critic. Perhaps because they are so corporeal. On the other hand, to call these fundamental human experiences the "central meanings" seems quite plausible for many people who have lived through them. In fact, the speaker's suggestion that these are *the* central meanings seems not sexually but *conceptually* provocative. Perhaps they are central meanings precisely because they are experiences that resist codified understanding to which we must submit. Perhaps they are central because they humble the part of human nature that would prefer to hover above experience, as a rational angel.

Here's Kirsch again, with a condescension for daily life that American poetry outgrew eighty years ago:

> Her poems are written directly out of the trivia of her life and can be directly assimilated by the reader; there is no abstraction and no surprise, only the videotape of life played back at full volume. . . . A reader of Olds is never made to question himself, only to congratulate himself on his fine sensitivity.

Kirsch's distaste for the poetry of the everyday is a replay of the aesthetic battle that Williams, Pound, and Eliot fought in the era of early modernism (and which was fought again in the fifties), about what the "proper" matter of poetry might be. There's no need to wage that war again: contemporary high-concept verse and domestic poetry coexist comfortably. As for the accusation of "simplicity," the only rebuttal required is to read a poem like "The Elder Sister" from Olds's *The Dead and the Living*:

> When I look at my elder sister now
> I think how she had to go first, down through the
> birth canal, to force her way
> head-first through the tiny channel,
> the pressure of Mother's muscles on her brain,
> the tight walls scraping her skin.
> Her face is still narrow from it, the long
> hollow cheeks of a Crusader on a tomb,
> and her inky eyes have the look of someone who has
> been in prison a long time and
> knows they can send her back. I look at her
> body and think how her breasts were the first to
> rise . . .
>   but now I
> see I had her before me always
> like a shield. I look at her wrinkles, her clenched
> jaws, her frown-lines—I see they are
> the dents on my shield, the blows that did not reach me.
> She protected me, not as a mother
> protects a child, with love, but as
> a hostage protects the one who makes her
> escape as I made my escape, with my sister's
> body held in front of me.

Merely literal? Lacking in surprise? In fact, "The Elder Sister," like many of Olds's poems, is a poem of complex recognitions: an exploration of memory, complicity, empathy, and power. As its reader, I'm not given to congratulate myself, nor do I think merely of my own family story. Rather, I consider how many intimate relationships are forged by the advantage of circumstance, and shaped by subconsciously consented-to pacts; that we are surrounded by barely submerged yet ignored dramas of competition, injustice, and power.

Kirsch seems to be oblivious to the complexity of metaphor, Olds's greatest gift. In "The Elder Sister," the rich intelligence of image welters up into a tangle of evocative association—*Crusader, tomb, brain, prisoner, shield, hostage*. To be more specific, consider the way that the "dents" on the speaker's "shield" echo the implied indentations on the sister's skull, left by her passage through the birth canal. The poetic nature of image is that it cross-pollinates, refracts, and echoes in ways that are quicker and stranger than rationality, evoking a host of intersecting contexts and subtexts that would take a discursive writer much longer to explicate.

Psychoanalysis may no longer function as a dominant paradigm in American poetry, as some have claimed, but its insights are not exhausted. In fact, those insights seem relevant to the vehement reactions of these two critics. As rite of passage in many societies, boys achieve manhood by striking their mothers and walking away, moving from a women's world into the male one. This is one way boys achieve autonomy, by pushing away the feminine and the corporeal. The desired consequence is essential: independence of self; but the side effect can be a lasting, anxious contempt for all things feminine.

It's no big revelation that misogyny is scripted so deeply into our cultural consciousness that it leaks out like radioactive fuel, but still, it is dismaying to see it dripping from the mandibles of the highly cultivated. Terror and embarrassment at the stuff of the body are quintessential symptoms of puritanism. Admittedly, a preference for abstraction and rationality over the less-controllable, corporeal, and emotional realms doesn't have to be neurotic. Yet the criticism so regularly showered on Olds seems just another form of the smirking treatment of the candidate Hillary Clinton in the political realm—the Rush Limbaughs and Bill O'Reillys, like apoplectic pit bulls of the commentating profession, alternately brand her a crybaby weakling and a ball-busting bitch.

Kirsch again, in his claim that Olds's sexual preoccupation is with scenarios of incest: "Across her six books, every permutation of this sin is played out: Olds imagines her parents having sex, and she imagines having sex with her parents, and imagines her children sexually." Kirsch goes on to quote from the poem "Saturn," in which Olds's drunken, stuporous father is imagined eating her younger brother:

> as he crunched the torso of his child between his jaws.
> crushed the bones like the soft shells of crabs
> and the delicacies of the genitals
> rolled back along his tongue . . .
> he could not
> stop himself, like orgasm.

Isn't this, again, not prurience but empathy, recognition, curiosity, and courage? Isn't one job of the artist to imagine his way vividly into the unfashionable nooks and crannies of experience, the central meanings of the real? I have always found the account in "Saturn" of the child-eating father a completely credible description of unconscious power, masculinity, and fathers. To me, this is not Olds's "prurient" imagination, but the real human story, embedded in myth and poetry, the tangle of primal psychological relationships. If this is an example of Olds's "prurience," then Ovid is a pervert, Dante a porno king, and *The Iliad* a splatter film made by a blind Italian director.

These literary antecedents are apt in other ways: all are practitioners of artistic luridity and excess, lovers of spectacle; in that sense, they too are "populists." Oscar Wilde said that all art is a matter of exaggeration, and when Homer narrates the slow-motion shot of a Trojan arrow piercing through three Greek bodies, we may complain about his sensationalism, but we don't avert our eyes. There's no question that Olds has a temperamental proclivity for shock, a somewhat insatiable drive for seeking and finding the taboo, the off-color, off-the-record, unsayable urges, sins, and behaviors of the human. A friend of mine says that Olds's poems are, in this way, like the paintings of Van Gogh: in their extremity of color and motion is a kind of vitality, a testimony to the life force to which the most unsophisticated viewer can respond.

Aside from the critique of her subject matter, the two critical accusations most recurrently leveled against Olds are those of repetition and craftlessness. In fact, though, Olds the poet has developed steadily in craft and style. Since her early books, she has conducted experiments that have largely gone unnoticed—forays toward greater lyric range and more subtle rhetorical strategies, sallies even into that notorious postmodern territory, "reflexivity."

As "The Elder Sister" shows, Olds's most elemental talent is metaphor, the intuitive intelligence of image; most impressively her genius has been for metaphor that describes and mirrors primal psychic relations. In "Why My Mother Made Me," for example, the speaker describes her mother looking at her infant "the way / the maker of a sword gazes at his face / in the steel of the blade." This fundamental poetic faculty has remained central to Olds's poetic strength. Yet real talent shifts and evolves over time. Over the years Olds has tested and enlarged her range to place more emphasis on diction, assonance and consonance, variety of idiom, and rhetoric.

In Olds's collection *One Secret Thing*, examples of such expanded ambitiousness are easy to find. In "Fly on the Wall in the Puritan Home," the poet literally imagines herself as an insect spectator, watching one human abuse another:

> And then I become a fly on the wall
> of that room, where the corporal punishment
> was done. The humans who are in it mean little
> to me . . .
> I turn my back and with maxillae and palps
> clean my arms: in each of the hundred
> eyes of both my compound eyes,
> one wallpaper rose. . . .
> . . . And my looking is a looking

primed, it is a looking to the power of itself,
and I see a sea folding inward,
200 little seas folding on themselves—
a mess of gene pool crushing down onto
its own shore. Then I turn back
to washing my hands of the chaff that flees off the
threshed onto the threshing floor.
Ho hum, I say, I'm just a fly—
fly light, fly bright, pieces of a species dashed
off onto a wall, chaff of wonder,
chaff of night.

The first thing to remark about "Fly on the Wall" is the sustained detachment of its point of view, a detachment of which the "emotionally identified" Olds, according to her critics, is supposed incapable. "The humans . . . mean little / to me," says the fly, and in fact, it is this clinical freedom of perspective that gives rise to some of the distinctive language and perceptions of the poem. Like the fly, the speaker here is "washing [her] hands" of human suffering, with "maxillae" and "palps."

The imagination of *seeing,* of the fly's penetrating vision, is another adventure here: of "looking / primed . . . looking to the power of itself," which sees one person hurting another as "a / mess of gene pool crushing down onto / its own shore." In themselves, these are ingenious conceptual descriptions. But there's a supporting drama of sound and tonal play in "Fly on the Wall" that also supplements and goes beyond straightforward narrative—"pieces of a species dashed," and "washing my hands of the chaff that flees off the / threshed onto the threshing floor." The strong assonance between *crushing, washing, threshed,* and *dashed off,* the internal rhyme, the bold verb choice of *flees*; the ingenious metaphor of *chaff* itself—all are reinforcing subtleties of craft.

The poem's conclusion especially demonstrates Olds's underappreciated rhetorical skills. It commences like a nursery rhyme: "Ho hum, I say, I'm just a fly," a tone that both sustains the poem's register of blithe animal indifference while guiding the story into a second tonal layer that soberly joins grotesque detail with dark, understated awe: "pieces of a species dashed / off onto a wall, chaff of wonder, / chaff of night." Terrifically inventive, wonderfully underplayed, this passage possesses the poetic quality Randall Jarrell called "original strangeness." And the effect seems not the least bit strained for.

A similar kind of nuanced fluency is visible in "Pansy Coda," which contradicts both Kirsch's and Logan's reductive summaries of Olds's poetic nature. For "Pansy Coda" is a poem of description, and though it dips sideways into a memory of the speaker's mother, it is principally an immersion in sensual seeing, a type of poem impossible to write without lyric resources:

> When I see them my knees get a little weak.
> I have to squat down close to them, I
> want to put my face in one of them.
> They are so buttery, and yet so clean.
> They have a kind of soaking-wet dryness,
> they have the tremulous chin, and the pair of
> ocular petals, and the pair of frail
> ear petals, the sweet dog face.
> Or is it like the vulva of a woman,
> or of some particular woman. My mother
> tended them—purple-black—
> when I kneel to them I am kneeling to my mother,
> . . . .
> . . . —I have no idea
> what she is thinking, I get that nervous feeling
> I've had all my life around my mother. But when I
> see a bed of these, I kneel,
> and gaze at each one, freshly and freshly wowed,
> I love to run my thumb softly
> over the gentle jaw, I would like
> to wrap myself in a cloak of them,
> a cloak of one if it were large enough.

I am tired of hating myself, tired
of loathing. I want to be carried in a petal
sling, sling of satin and cream,
I want to be dazed, I want the waking sleep.

It doesn't seem so far-fetched to be reminded of Whitman's "What is the grass" passage, or Lawrence's "Bavarian Gentians" when reading this beautiful, erotically descriptive lyric. Both delicacy and strength are alternately employed, with the easy grace of someone who has spent a lifetime shaping language. Here, perceptual generosity is extended not to the "narcissistic" self, nor to the algebras of sex, but to the pansies. The progress of the poem itself recapitulates Olds's development as a poet, from the appealing plainness of the first three lines, to the movement into rich and various metaphor, then its gradual progress into a kind of chanting lyricism. There's the fantastically casual, ingenious, and relaxed moment of "I kneel, / and gaze at each one, freshly and freshly wowed." Then arrives the brilliant, surprising, and intuitively believable last lines, which unite Eros and Thanatos in the most convincing manner. I leave it to any lover of poetry to say that "Pansy Coda" is not a subtle and masterfully made poem.

Olds's later collections are not a dramatic breakthrough into a new aesthetic era for the poet. They contain the same array of poetic styles and strategies she has employed for some time: many of the poems are about family and bodies; many open with the word "When," which situates them in a narrative time and place, setting up a frame for the imaginative explorations that are her specialty. That she doesn't seem to care about not repeating herself, or about impressing critics, seems obvious. Yet Olds is occasionally an extraordinary poet—not just one possessed of a talent for great empathetic insight (nothing to scoff at), but also one of impressive poetic means. Some poets simply produce a lot of poems because they must, and because they can. Their surplus is part of what enables them to make the truly good pieces. It seems foolish and ungrateful to fault for surfeit a poet who has given us many, many extraordinary poems.

Although Olds has recently received the serious recognitions of the Pulitzer Prize, and the British T. S. Eliot Prize, it is likely that our reception of Sharon Olds as a poet has been arrested, our perception petrified and sealed itself into a version of our first encounter with that work. Often that early encounter was of a family narrative, leading to an imagistically mediated psychological revelation. It's the oppression of habit that makes even her freshest new poems seem already known to us. And it's a misbegotten nervousness about our own literary sophistication that causes us to label her as a "middlebrow" poet, or to be silent about our affection for her work. In fact, any contemporary poet with an ounce of sense would feel lucky to have written as many scintillating poems as Olds, and to have moved so many readers. The jealousy and dustups over the ultimate worth of her poems will continue, but will eventually settle, and we'll see them for what they are—an extended, meticulous, passionate, often deeply meditative testament about the "central meanings"; skilled dramatic expressions of the most archetypal templates, obstructions and liberations of one human life. This is not a matter of "high" and "low" culture. The dismissiveness of some critics only indicates the resistance that still exists to the news Olds carries: consciousness and unconsciousness, body and soul, swim in the same water, and they don't like each other. Fortunate for us to have poets like Olds to preside over the endless negotiations.

Soul Radio:
Marie Howe, Jane Hirshfield, and Linda Gregg

In our odd contemporary moment, when, in some corners, poetic directness and sincerity are cause for aesthetic embarrassment, the so-called spiritual poet runs pronounced risks. The manners of the day are more disposed to obliquity than testimony, and the straightforward urge toward wisdom is considered a rather unsophisticated undertaking for poetry. Most poets under forty are more comfortable telling it slant, with a twist, than speaking directly of faith. If all signs only point to other signs, and if meaning infinitely recedes as we approach, what is the object of pursuit?

The works of so-called wisdom poets, such as Lucille Clifton, or Jane Kenyon, or Carl Dennis, or Sharon Olds, or Stephen Dunn, or William Stafford, or W. S. Merwin, or Galway Kinnell, aren't taught in many MFA programs; such poems aren't, perhaps, viewed as *difficult* enough to need smart people to explain them. Against a postmodern background, the sincerity of such poets must seem, well, touchingly simplistic. After all, there isn't enough time in the semester to visit and examine the obvious! In the corridors of higher education, where intellect is often self-regarding and self-perpetuating, official artistic value often seems to be assigned on the basis of aesthetic difficulty.

Moreover, such poets renew our confusions about the categorical blur between art and spirituality, between poets and "teachers," between poems and gospels, between artists and seekers. That confusion is understandable. The true believer and the artist are like twins separated at birth—each has a quarrel with the world; each has an instinct to seek the universal. They traffic in the same vocabulary: *heart, soul, sorrow, light, dark, death*. Both types are trying to get at the ineffable; each points toward unnoticed registers of experience, which might enrich us. It's easy to conflate, and not always natural to seg-regate the two. We are devotional creatures, and sacred texts are our earliest poetry.

Perhaps the telling distinction between the spiritualist and the poet has to do with a difference in goal. The poet, unlike the seeker, is not trying to *get* somewhere, or to improve herself. It's called *The Pilgrim's Progress*, after all, not *The Poet's Progress*. Poets are not dedi-cated to self-purification. Nor is all poetry, not by any means, aiming for the transcendental. Stanley Kunitz used to say that young poets should not try to resolve but to amplify and intensify their own inner contradictions; such polarities constitute the essential dramatic mate-rials of poem making. Don't increase peace; instead, refine strife. Not an orthodox spiritual program.

Nonetheless, we have a stubborn appetite, and ample motive, for raising consciousness. We may be less fervent in the postmodern era, less declarative, and more privatized in our devotions, but there are still plenty of seekers around. American Buddhism, the pragmatic gospel of Twelve Step programs, the multiple subcultures of New Age spirituality—their flourishing is evidence of an ongoing allegiance to the Big Thirst. Increasingly deprived of viable traditional institutions, we are still believers.

Which brings us to poetry. In a secular time, especially, poetry is always going to be a conservancy for articulations of human faith; a protected wetlands, a nondenominational land trust for prayer and ceremony. Secular or sacred in form, poems are one place in which the ongoing instinct for sacrament and for relationship to the eternal is sought, expressed, explored, grounded, and represented.

Three distinct precincts of spirit are to be found in the work of Marie Howe, Jane Hirshfield, and Linda Gregg. In a time when "directness" is unfashionable, they take the risk of addressing matters of faith. In their respective ways, their attention is resolutely intent on making contact with Being. Moreover, their American individualities are influenced by religious traditions of striking diversity. Respectively, they might be loosely aligned with American versions of Catholic, Buddhist, and Greek ecstatic vision.

What characterizes these poets as more "spiritual" than any other? To start with, a familiarity with states of grace, and the priority they give to their pursuit of it. What constitutes grace differs among them; their descriptions of it and their manners of approach vary considerably. For Hirshfield, grace has to do with attunement of mind; for Howe, with an intuition of being blessed, which in a Christian context implies a higher power; for Gregg, communion is a pagan, almost violent experience—the affirmation of a wild power running through and underneath the world.

The potential aesthetic pitfalls of so-called spiritual poetry are well known—didacticism, piety, pretentiousness, and sentimentality. Such risks accompany the undertaking. In fact, each of these poets sometimes drifts toward preachiness or aloofness, preciousness or didacticism. Yet their best poems are full of subtlety, discrimination, and power. Each in her own way gets at matters difficult to locate— spiritually elusive, existentially subtle, and hard to articulate. Only a seeker would find them, and only a poet-seeker would succeed in the art of framing them.

Their common ground is also substantial—most evident perhaps in their allegiance to the plain style, the linguistic equivalent of homemade cloth. These are poets of clarity, and they write in speech accessible to almost any reader. Likewise, there is an unspoken austerity in the worlds that they present, as if sumptuousness of detail, as well as opulence of word, would be beside the point. In their poems one finds no Concorde jets or sushi bars, no analogies to the tennis court, and very little Italian statuary. Obviously, all three are women poets, and one might well wonder at the gender demographics of American spirituality.

Though Gregg, Howe, and Hirshfield may stylistically forswear evident sophistication, each is a skilled rhetorician, employing forceful grammatical and logical structures to pressurize and inflect the stakes of the everyday. They are fearless of abstract declaration. Although they are direct, they are not reductive. Each is, in a different way, an ecstatic poet, drawn toward the poetic analogue of an altered state of consciousness.

Marie Howe

Marie Howe's poems are so natural seeming, her readers might mistakenly think poetry is as easy as ordinary speech. Her work also makes a case for the artistic value of a religious education. Howe is a lyric narrativist, a teller of exemplary stories, but what distinguishes her work from that of other quasi-confessional poets is her deep intuitive grasp of myth. Of the poets discussed here, Howe is the one who carries the Christian myths internally.

It is this symbolic understructure—in Howe's case, a cosmology drawn from Catholic Christianity—that lends her not a subject matter so much as a mythic idiom. All religious systems—Christian, Muslim, Sufi—are archetype in motion and their symbolic systems empower the imagination. Howe's poems seem traced over deep archetypal narratives of grief, sacrifice, choice, and grace. Yet they rarely seem willful, artificed, or acquiescent to a learned trope. Howe's instincts are formed, or you could say, awakened, by religious imagination, not subordinated to it.

Howe is best known for her second book, *What the Living Do,* whose narrative poems review the death of her brother John from AIDS. The many deathbed vignettes are oblique gospels, which the speaker shapes to poetry. The beginning of "The Gate" is an example:

> I had no idea that the gate I would step through
> to finally enter this world
>
> would be the space my brother's body made. He was
> a little taller than me.

"He died that I might live": the story is central for Howe, and her formulation of it is the very one that underlies Christianity. The symbolic sacrifice of the son/brother, and the realization of grace in the wake of loss—this is one of Howe's key scriptures. But Howe is so skillful at the alignment of her stories with parable and archetype that a reader hardly notices.

Howe's artlessness is also exerted on other parts of the family story. Many of her poems are set in the family house, which is the house of the father. In "The Boy," for instance, the speaker tells the story of her brother expelled from the household, exiled for his long hair. Tricked by a false promise from the father, he returns, is shorn, and leaves again, angry and estranged. On the surface, "The Boy" is an average family drama from the long-haired sixties; yet the narrative elements seem as old as human culture: the symbol of shorn hair, the father's banishment of the son, the son in self-chosen exile—these motifs exude such antique resonance. In "The Boy," Howe draws out more peripheral, contemporary, and less scripturally explored resonances of gender. At the poem's conclusion, the speaker, having failed to reconcile the men, is the one who sees the rigidities of gender prophetically inscribed in the story:

> What happened in our house taught my brothers how to leave,
> how to walk
> down a sidewalk without looking back.
>
> I was the girl. What happened taught me to follow him, whoever
> he was,
> calling and calling his name.

The fingerprints of scripture are all over this, but so are the stories of Narcissus and Echo, Orpheus and Eurydice. These primal mythic narratives resonate in deep alignment with the contemporary tale. Howe almost always feels marvelously natural and reliable in the mythic access of her poems.

Such poems at their best thrill us with their deep structure, whether we recognize its sources or not; for more self-conscious readers, they renew our recognition of the value, and the unavoidability, of the old stories. What is a poem but an echo chamber? Our stories, and human experience itself, are more fundamental and unchanging than we think. There's a profound reassurance in such continuity.

Howe's imagination is also intensely communal in orientation. She instinctively leans toward constructions of tribe. Her affirmations of the human condition are collective, variously including communities of family, gender, faith, and place. In her third collection, *The Kingdom of Ordinary Time,* the poet extends her range beyond the death/redemption chords of her earlier stories; as the title suggests, Howe's topic has become Time—the responsibility of incarnation, how to enter it willingly, not to deny it. "No Going Back might be the name of that angel," says the speaker in "Mary (Reprise)"; "—no more reverie." Here the poet configures herself as the Mary of Renaissance painting, awakened by divine summons, and irrevocably changed, her place in the book she is reading permanently lost. Howe's vision is both delicate and firm in application. "Let it be done to me, Mary finally said, and that / was the last time, for a long time, that she spoke about the past." Here, as in her earlier work, Howe's cosmology of grace has the familiar but not simpleminded Christian superstructure: fate is an unknowable combination of volition, cooperation, and divine intervention.

The Kingdom of Ordinary Time also shows some new resources in Howe's handling of tone and treatment; humor, not previously a notable presence in her poems, now pops up in freshets, as in the beginning of "Reading Ovid":

> The thing about those Greeks and Romans is that
> at least mythologically,
>
> they could get mad. If the man broke your heart, if he
> fucked your sister speechless

then real true hell broke loose:
> "You know that stew you just ate for dinner, honey?—

It was your son."
> That's Ovid for you.

This is delightful, and its sassy, profane lexicon is unexpected in Howe's writing: "fucked," "those Greeks," "they could get mad." The poem later assumes more meditative formality, but one feels new pleasures and potential enlivening Howe's work.

When, in *Ordinary Time,* the poet sometimes aims for political assertions, her touch is more fallible, and sometimes forced. Speaking of Afghanistan or American imperialism, the lines can fall flat. The vision that comes most naturally to Howe is the familial: the bonds and betrayals of brotherhood, friendship, and the fraught relations between women and men. Since the variations on those dynamics are endless, one knows that Howe has material to last a lifetime.

One of the best pieces in the book is "The Snow Storm," an effortless-seeming poem in which an unpretentious pastoral landscape, colored by the speaker's scriptural vision, is transformed into a nuanced and evocative parable. The whole poem follows:

> I walked down towards the river, and the deer had left tracks
> deep as half my arm, that ended in a perfect hoof
> and the shump shump sound my boots made walking
> > made the silence loud.

> And when I turned back towards the great house
> I walked beside the deer tracks again.
> And when I came near the feeder: little tracks of the birds on
>   the surface
> > of the snow I'd broken through.

> *Put your finger here, and see my hands, then bring your*
> > *hand and put it in my side.*

> I put my hand down into the deer track
>> and touched the bottom of an invisible hoof.
> Then my finger in the little mark of the jay.

"Put your finger here," says the Christ to the doubting Thomas, and, like a mime in a dream, the speaker in the poem puts her hand down into the tracks of the animals—and finds what? Signs and wonders, evidence of a world that is invisible but real, both inside and outside time; the communion of creaturely existence. The integration in "The Snow Storm" of the natural world with the mythologies of faith is rich and exciting; but the plot also reminds us of the Christian construct: that the world is the house of the father, in which the speaker, doubter though she may be, wanders.

"The Snow Storm" is a magical and effortless evocation of the faith test and of redemption from beyond, rendered with no cant, explication, or didacticism. Such enviable naturalness seems to illustrate how in tune the believer is with several worlds at once, connected by insight and echo. Howe's delicate touch makes it new again. The nature of doubters (which all of us are) demands that grace has to be contacted, checked, and contracted, again and again. The most modest revelations, signs, and wonders remind us, as Emerson said, that we are in the lap of a vast Intelligence. As Emerson also said, the poet is the sensitive medium for the community at large.

Jane Hirshfield

In some odd universe (ours), Jane Hirshfield has become the poetry face of American Buddhism. Like Howe, Hirshfield employs a plain vocabulary and plenty of declaration in concert with elements of image and narrative. Hirshfield's work does as much "telling" as Howe's, but is almost never familial. The substantial difference is that Hirshfield's world is not about *community* but the path of the solitary seeker. In ways related to her Buddhist metaphysics, Hirshfield's poems are more introspective and elusive. Howe's poems tend to frame their speaker poised on the dramatic edge of the self, inside

a moment when something demands to be known. Hirshfield likewise often writes from the fulcrum of a moment, but one less in-
trinsically dramatized. In many senses of the word, Hirshfield is a
more "indoor" poet. Howe's speaker is clarified and authorized by
momentary illuminations of the grace in dailiness. In Hirshfield's
Buddhism-influenced poems, the speaker is on her own: a gentler
kind of revelation is sought. Take the unmomentous beginning of the
poem called "It Was Like This":

> It was like this:
> you were happy, then you were sad,
> then happy again, then not.
>
> It went on.

In this poem and others, Hirshfield seeks an alternative to the "ah
ha" breakthrough moment of epiphany that has informed so much
poetry—the breakthrough that echoes either the experience of therapeutic insight or sexual climax. Instead, the calm recitation of fact represents the repetitive, nondramatic actuality of most experience.
Hirshfield's method is one of catch-and-release insight.

Her great theme is ignorance, or "not-knowing," and how it is paradoxically related to aliveness. As a Buddhist, Hirshfield relishes and
cultivates ignorance as the precondition of authentic experience. It's a
rich subject, and surely many poets have handled it, but few with the
resourcefulness or steady intentness of Hirshfield. That theme is lucid
in the poem "Moment":

> A person wakes from sleep
> and does not know for a time
> who she is, who he is.
>
> This happens in a lifetime
> once or twice.
> It has happened to you, no doubt.

Some in that moment
panic,
some sigh with pleasure.

How each kind later envies the other,
who must so love their lives.

For all its plainness, "Moment" shows the kind of perfect machine Hirshfield can construct. The paradox of the poem—that this experience of "not-knowing self" can provoke opposite but equal reactions in different individuals—is sad, benevolent, and humorous. All things, the poem suggests, are true at once; the dance of subjectivity is rich and paradoxical. Even the manufacture of unnecessary suffering, a frequent product of human nature, is part of the dance.

"Moment" exposes another characteristic dimension of Hirshfield's sensibility; she is a student, not of specific perceptions (her poems are not, on their own, all that *sensuous*), but of *stances* toward perception. Her poems focus on the manner in which perception is turned into conception. "Moment" infers how an instant of nonidentity can as easily be experienced as freedom as anxiety. It's a matter of subliminal choice. One person's experience of "emptiness" can be another's "spaciousness."

Cognition is preconditioned, say the sutras. Therefore, "distinctions matter," as Hirshfield says in her poem "After Long Silence," which continues: "Whether a goat's / quiet face should be called noble / or indifferent. The difference between a right rigor and pride." Hirshfield's poems focus on the consequence of even casual assumptions, and her best poems are finely tuned constructs of implication, which poise readers on a brink of making or unmaking an understanding of their own. The rigorous indirectness of the koan tradition seems an integral part of her poetic craft.

Hirshfield's poems frequently arrive at insight through a sequence of propositions and riddles. They take as a premise that the mind needs to be baited into insight, needs coaxing to slip the knot of its own knowing. Thus, one of Hirshfield's most admirable skills is implication. She makes discriminating use of the unspoken; the arts of reticence, inference, and paradox. She likes, as the poem "Moment" suggests, her statements to cut back against the grain of each other, Venn diagram–style, as a way of isolating some small area of experience or concept. She is a great "focuser." At its best, this dialectical method requires an intuitive participation and subtlety from the reader. Paradox, cross-eyed cousin to logic, is central to Hirshfield's dialectical method.

In "Muslin," even common assumptions about Buddhist-like practices of "detachment" and "acceptance" are scrutinized. The speaker tells of a friend who has a romantic relationship with a come-and-go lover (who might be thought of as "unreliable"). In explanation, her friend asks her, "Do you ask the weather why it comes or goes?" The poem's underlying question is whether such idealistic nonattachment is possible or even desirable in a romantic human context? Second, is the speaker critical, or jealous of her friend? What's impressive about the poem is that it avoids the reductiveness of either ethical or personal resolution. The poem ends without resolving its question:

> She was lovely, my friend, even the gray
> of her hair was lovely. A listening rope-twist
> half pity, half envy tightened its length in my chest.
> . . . .
> The hands on her lap seemed quiet,
> even contented.
> I noticed something unspoken begin to
>
> billow and shimmer between us,
> weightless as muslin,
> but neither of us moved to lift it away.

Hirshfield's best poems conjure this kind of intuitive thrill in the resonance of what's unsaid; the artfulness lies in the indirectness with which the trump card is delivered. Hirshfield's strength as a poet lies in the subtle housings that she constructs for the intellect. Because the preceding puzzle has been so nicely constructed, there's something very pleasant about the inconclusiveness of the closing image of "Muslin." Like an open cage with something invisible inside, the poem catches the irresolvability of experience, our inability to actually judge life from its midst. One intuits that attachment and disattachment are each challenging in its own way. With such an aesthetic of attentiveness applied to experience, a quiet moment may be as tricky and dramatic as a thunderstorm. The main thing, says the Buddha, is to stay tuned for ongoing developments.

Because of its emphasis on cognition itself, and its nuanced descriminations, Hirshfield's work can seem somewhat dispassionate at times. The most telling criticism one could make of her work is that the speaker rarely seems out of control. Nonetheless, Hirshfield mostly succeeds in her delivery of news about life, expressed with forceful but not simplistic simplicity. The poem "It Was Like This" concludes:

> It doesn't matter what they will make of you
> or your days: they will be wrong.
> . . . .
> Your story was this: you were happy, then you were sad,
> you slept, you awakened.
> Sometimes you ate roasted chestnuts, sometimes persimmons.

Hirshfield risks plainness, and the lover of sumptuous language will not find his heart's desire here. Still, Hirshfield's emphasis on our condition of ignorance—and its paradoxical celebration—is unusual in American poetry. Spare as they are, Hirshfield's best poems hold a lot of space inside them. The emphasis on mystery itself is a distinctive aesthetic ambition, and to an unusual degree, Hirshfield's poems place trust in the reader's deductive intelligence.

Linda Gregg

If Howe is a mystic Christian of American poetry, and Hirshfield an American koan engineer, Linda Gregg could be said to represent an equally old literary lineage from another culture—the Greek Way, in which grief, Eros, and ecstasy are indissoluble. In her stylistic plainness, austerity, and directness, it's quite fitting to place Gregg in the orbital of Howe and Hirshfield. But Gregg's spirituality is more stark and passionate, more erotic, carnal, and fatal than those cousin-poets, and her lyrics are run through with a streak of tragic extremism. Gregg finds grace in ruination, and gives herself to delirium, with an immodesty outside the range of the contemplative Hirshfield or the pilgrim Howe.

In this temperamental way, Gregg is also kin to immodest dramatists like Akhmatova and Sappho, those enthusiasts of ruin, given to abjectness and heroism, who hurl themselves on the bonfire of passion with relish. The poem "Etiology" illustrates:

> Cruelty made me. Cruelty and the sweet smelling earth,
> and the wet scent of boy. The heave in the rumps
> of horses galloping. Heaven forbid that my body not
> perish with the rest. I have smelled the rotten wood
> after rain and watched maggots write on
> dead animals. I have lifted the dead owl while it
> was still warm. Heaven forbid that I should be saved.

Gregg is a bona fide pagan poet, and the reader can sense the authority of very old cultural traditions behind her manners, manners married to a fierce intensity. Hers is an earth religion, a fleshed-and-blooded spirituality, distinct from the epiphany seeking of the Transcendentalist, or the contemplative nuancing of Buddhism:

> As long as I struggle to float above the ground
> and fail, there is reason for this poetry.
> . . . .
> . . . See me rise like a flame,
> like the sun, moon, stars, birds wind. In light.
> In dark. But I never achieve it. I get on my knees
> this gray April to see if open crocuses have a smell.

I must live in the suffering and desire of what
rises and falls. The terrible blind grinding
of gears against our bodies and lives.

("It Is the Rising I Love")

The temerity required to write lines like "It Is the Rising I Love" or "I Am One Chosen by the Lion" (the title and first line of another poem), poems that don't *reason* with the mysteries of god, suffering or life, is one of Gregg's representative strengths: she swings for the fence. Her voice presumes a Delphic authority, a confidence that her speaker's passion is not merely personal but also sacramental, representative of the human condition. When a poem succeeds, what comes across is a kind of chin-raised-high nobility, joined to a blunt directness.

Elsewhere, in poems of her quieter self, Gregg can leave declamation behind and speak with a serene factuality, as in "Summer in a Small Town":

When the men leave me,
they leave me in a beautiful place.
It is always late summer.
When I think of them now,
I think of the place.
And being happy alone afterwards.
This time it's Clinton, New York
I swim in the public pool
at six when the other people
have gone home.
The sky is grey, the air hot.
I walk back across the mown lawn
loving the smell and the houses
so completely it leaves my heart empty.

"Small Town" represents the other side of Gregg's talent: understatement, attentiveness, simplicity. Here sensuous data and tone do

their own connotative work. And, as the poem suggests, an unpretentious and satisfying feminism runs through Gregg's work—an ongoing meditation about the destinies and privilege of gender. As often
as these poems are about abandonment, they usually reach abandonment's other shore—the sufficiency and pleasures of solitary life, as in
the gorgeous poem "The Color of Many Deer Running":

> The air fresh, as it has been for days.
> Upper sky lavender. Deer on the far hill.
> The farm woman said they would be gone
> when I got there as I started down the lane.
> Jumped the stream. Went under great eucalyptus
> where the ground was stamped bare by two bulls
> who watched from the other side of their field.
> The young deer were playing as the old ate
> or guarded. Then all were gone, leaping.
> Except one looking down from the top.
> The ending made me glad. I turned toward
> the red sky and ran back down to the farm,
> the man, the woman, and the young calves.
> Thinking that as I grow older I will lose
> my color. Will turn tan and gray like the deer.
> Not one deer, but when many of them run away.

To be sure, Gregg's visionary impulses don't always succeed as
poems. At their less than best, Gregg's pagan priestess mode can seem
excessively posed. She overuses the sentence fragment, as a means to
impart drama to perceptions that they don't necessarily earn. Joined
with Gregg's fondness for grand abstraction, the result can seem melo-
dramatic, or inflated, as in "The Bounty after the Bounty":

> It is all not in having.
> A mountain of three goddesses
> without goddesses. Where they had been.

Gone, but truer therefore.
The absence, the loss creates a truth.
They go away but something remains.
They remain. It is their absence that I find,
that hold onto.
Having is the mistaken focus of desire.
It is not the point.

Unrelieved by tonal alteration, and uninformed by story or description, such passages can come off as arid or pretentious—too much drama and not enough cargo. When extreme abstraction, weak syntax, and an imperious tone are combined like this, it seems like an attempt to capitalize on pitch rather than substance.

We should remember, though, that poets necessarily risk self-importance in order to make real poems. Presumption is truly part of their job description, a trait as necessary for modernists and formalists as for romantics. The high-chivalric side of Gregg's poetry, even when stiff seeming, is impressive for its temerity and intensity.

Gregg's poems, whether inhabiting the oracular mode or the contrastingly plain voice, also show an instinct for paradox, which convincingly contrasts the yearning for transcendence and the pressures of convention, denying the validity of neither. In the poem "I Thought on His Desire for Three Days," the speaker unrepentantly recounts some details of an adulterous affair. The speaker's transcendence of regret comes from an appreciation for the paradoxes of human life, and a certainty that some truths defy logic, ethics, or common sense. Such a stance can find exultation even in ruin or failure:

> In Chicago,
> a police siren ran through my heart even though
> it was not for me. I was strong. I knew where
> I was. I knew what I had achieved. When the wife
> called and said I was a whore, I was quiet,
> but inside I said "perhaps." It has been raining

all night. Summer rain. The liveliness of it keeps
me awake. I am so happy to have lived.

There's something fundamentally believable about this fatalistic
ecstasy, this insight that puts us in touch with the laws of both above
and below, both the secret soul and our damaged, damaging lives
in time.

In *All of It Singing: New and Selected Poems,* Gregg often manages to
tell the truth in what Yeats called "the high old way." When her poems
hit their sweet spot, they strike a note that is both tragic and reverent;
they display an acceptance of fate that seems clean and valuable as a
reference point, as well as elegant in language. The directness of such
work enlarges our perspective, makes us more honest, and perhaps
even more willing to encounter our own experience at a new depth. It
is one of the old accomplishments for which poetry exists.

Contemplating the poetics of Howe, Hirshfield, and Gregg, one notices
how much presumption, in our era, simplicity requires—how much
confidence, or is it conviction, or is it necessity?—is required to aim
for wisdom; to seek the way inside appearances and beyond transience.
So much poetry now has lowered the stakes, settling for the habits of
beauty. Far more poets strive to be manic, evasive, or heuristically
sophisticated than simple. Difficulty is their way of claiming member-
ship in postmodernity. A spiritual poet is one who seeks alignment with
the laws of creation; with that which is both part of and beyond the
human. In our era, even to remember that such parameters exist is difficult when the priority and scale of the man-made proclaims itself from
every TV and cell phone conversation.

These poets who follow the insight track risk seeming pretentious
to some and being ignored by many others. In central Colorado, I met
the town librarian of a small town; he has, he told me, on his own,
started memorizing poems. What poems? I asked. Wallace Stevens
and Jane Kenyon. Standing under the giant dusty cottonwoods in the
town park, he recited Jane Kenyon's "Happiness" to me. It was beautiful.

Any practicing poet who believes that small ceremony of art was a
fluke, or insignificant, or who thinks that Kenyon's poem isn't part of
the tribal treasure, is fooling him- or herself. A little hardship, a little
sickness, a little mourning, a little failure, a lost job or broken marriage
will quickly clarify for us the function of poetry. Vale of tears, oh un-
real city; dark world. Meet poetry.

The Village Troublemaker:
Robert Bly and American Poetry

I once saw Robert Bly ruin the evening for a whole auditorium full of happy people. This was in the seventies, in Fairfield, Iowa, a small town fifty miles south of the University of Iowa, where I was an undergraduate. On the bulletin board at the health food store, I had seen an advertisement—*Robert Bly* was going to read his poems at Maharishi International University in Fairfield! And so, three of us drove down: I, my sort-of girlfriend, Lynn, and my friend Dave. It was one of those moonless winter nights, a deep oppressive dark around the road, making our tiny car headlights seem solitary and perishable. Midwest deep winter nights, like those in the Northeast, can be suffocating in their gloom, malevolent and unnatural seeming.

Now I remember that it must have been icy, because, halfway there, when a deer appeared in the middle of the highway, and I braked, our car slewed and skidded. We hit the deer anyway, a big doe, with a solid *thunk*. It went down and skidded on its side out in front of us, like a hockey puck, about twenty feet. Then there was the smash of silence that follows such an event, and the woman in the passenger seat, weeping, with her face in her hands, as we sat there.

The deer, however, was not done for. After a minute, it hoisted itself up, found its legs, then gigantically leaped across one of the roadside ditches, out into the white black snowy fields.

Maharishi International University in Fairfield was a tidy little campus in the middle of a small town in the middle of nowhere. Does anyone anymore, as they say in the Midwest, remember the Maharishi? The one with the long stringy gray hair, and beard? The guru who taught the Beatles to meditate in India? His Transcendental Meditation was one of the first guru franchises in the United States. For fifty dollars you could be issued a personal Sanskrit mantra, a lesson in its application, and a meditator's union card. And if you wanted to get a degree in TM science, or mathematics, or engineering, or art, you could (and still can) enroll at Maharishi University.

It was around that time that rumors and news articles reported that some Transcendental meditators were "flying": able to actually rise from the ground with their cultivated yogic powers. A few photographs in circulation showed them, like blurry UFOs, hovering six inches above their sitting cushions.

Fairfield, Iowa, one senses, may have been chosen for the isolation it provided. The nice New Englandy brick buildings, the glass-walled library, the well-kept grounds—the facilities seemed a little eerie, like a movie set, or a facsimile of a college campus. This effect was enhanced by the many Maharishi students and faculty present at the reading: fresh-faced people who seemed excessively cheerful and friendly, as if in possession of a secret beyond the ken of civilians. Maybe they were just being nice; on the other hand, maybe they were acting on orders from the public relations department.

That night, however, Mr. Bly wasn't in the mood for bliss. Well over six feet, bulky of girth, with an unkempt rooster comb of thick dark hair, he stood on stage at the front of the auditorium, in a Peruvian serape, and, for two hours, alternately read poems and harangued the crowd. He would finish a poem, and look up at the audience of a hundred or so, "Why are you smiling?!" he would say. "Why are you smiling? Do you think that that poem is funny? You look ridiculous. I've never seen such a zoo full of grinning monkeys! You can't be happy unless you know the darkness inside yourself. If you're a human being, you don't get to skip steps! Are you human?"

Not knowing what else to do, confused, the audience of cheerful Transcendentalists helplessly continued to grin, grimly hanging on to their smiles as he flayed them like paint stripper. "Now I'm going to read a poem by Rilke. This is about the loneliness a man feels that has spent his life in the wrong way."

> All of you undisturbed cities,
> haven't you ever longed for the Enemy?
> I'd like to see you besieged by him
> for ten endless and ground-shaking years.
>
> Until you were desperate and mad with suffering;
> finally in hunger you would feel his weight.
> He lies outside the walls like a countryside.
> And he knows very well how to endure
> longer than the ones he comes to visit.
> . . . .
> He is the one who breaks down the walls,
> and when he works, he works in silence.

In the etiquette of the poetry reading, sanctum of mandatory, reverential silence, I don't believe I had ever seen a performance like this. Without a hint of ambivalence, Bly played the role of rogue shaman, the stranger from afar, who, invited inside the city walls, insults his host, turns over the dining room table, threatens and browbeats the bureaucrats; the most contrarian of preachers.

Bly's mode has always been combative. Throughout his adult life, he has pushed things and people around, in a style some would call brash, others heroic. His lifelong engagement with American culture at large, and with poetry culture in particular, has been opinionated and often ferocious. One gets the sense that fighting is, for Bly, a way of finding things out, of trial by battery and head butting. For fifty years he has attacked whatever establishment has caught his attention, from the American government's "military-industrial complex" in the sixties, to the Iowa Writers' Workshop (which he attended), to Western rationality and consumerism, to the dementia of masculine patriarchy. Retrospectively, what is surprising is how intuitive and worthwhile his opinions have been.

One can get the flavor of Bly's sweeping style of pronouncement by peering into any of his essays. Here's what he says in his 1963 jeremiad, "A Wrong Turning in American Poetry":

In American poetry . . . a young poet cannot take on Pound, Eliot, or Moore for a master without severe distortion of his own personality. They whirl about so far out that anyone who follows them will freeze to death. If American poetry has a center it would seem to be William Carlos Williams. His poetry, however, shows a fundamental absence of spiritual intensity.

"Spiritual intensity" is the measuring stick he has insisted upon as an essential poetic value, and it is a characteristic of Bly himself. Bly has been poetry's village bigmouth, our Norman Mailer, our Noam Chomsky. To look at the man's life, poems, and career is to see, by contrast, how provincial most American poetry is; how limited in its chosen range of influence and in its ambition; how self-referential.

The American mentality finds these mixed allegiances contradictory. Since high modernism separated artistic culture from mainstream culture in the early twentieth century, we tend to polarize these different parts of life; we practice not just separation of church and state but separation of politics, spirituality, and aesthetic life. We suppose that artists should be specialists, bohemian and quirky, self-involved and self-enclosed. We forget that the great pragmatist William James loved séances; the very political Yeats spent evenings with a Ouija board and hung out with Madame Blavatsky; and Jean Toomer went from the Harlem Renaissance to study Sufic dancing in France with Gurdjieff.

Truthfully, Bly's career has had so many developments and phases, so many directions, and causes, it is hard to summarize, but two preoccupations are visible throughout: first, his refusal to segregate the political, the artistic, and the spiritual; and second, his ongoing certainty about the human value of the irrational imagination. In his seminal manifesto for radical associative poetry, the book *Leaping Poetry*, he summarizes his version of the Western tradition:

Sometime in the thirteenth century poetry in Europe began to show a distinct decline in the ability to associate powerfully. . . . By

the eighteenth century . . . freedom of association had become drastically curtailed. . . . The poet's thought plodded through the poem,
line after line, like a man being escorted through a prison. . . . This
careful routing of psychic energy . . . had a crippling effect upon the
psychic life.

One of the places Bly has repeatedly sought that spiritual intensity
and inspiration is in the poetry of other cultures. "If we keep our eyes
too closely on poetry in English," he wrote in 1958, "we see, when we
look for something new, nothing but Eliot, Pound, Williams, and others, but if we look abroad we see some astonishing landscapes: the
Spanish tradition of Neruda, and Vallejo; the Swedish tradition of
Ekelof; in the French, Char and Michaux, in the German, Trakl and
Benn . . . all of them writing in the new imagination."

Bly's translation work alone would constitute a major contribu-
tion to twentieth-century literature: Neruda, Vallejo, Lorca, Machado,
Rilke, Tranströmer, Kabir, Rumi, Hafez, and on and on; if Bly was not
the first American to bring these poets into American literature, he
was the first to popularize them, in part through his clear, idiomatic
translations. His magazine, whose title changed from *The Fifties* to *The
Sixties* to *The Seventies,* laid out an agenda of imaginative expansion
and engagement for American poetry, and emphasized the importance of poets in translation; he imported their energy into American
poetry. What is more, he invented a way of talking about such poets, a
style that is boisterous and non-academic, but discriminating. "There
is an imagination," he says, "which assembles the three kingdoms
within one poem: the dark figures of politics, the world of streetcars,
and the ocean world."

It's hard to imagine what American poetry would be like today if
not for this wholesale importation of riches from afar. The influences,
subject matter, and technical resources of Vallejo, Tranströmer, Rilke,
and Kabir have been absorbed, transformed, and passed through three
generations of American poets already; in ways that many aren't aware
of, we owe a giant debt to Bly and his comrades in that effort.

The Power of the Image

A public intellectual who prizes the irrational; a political activist with spiritual instincts; an internationalist who applies Jung to historical analysis: these diverse engagements are, in the Bly aesthetic, all facilitated through a particular poetic technology, the *image*. The term *deep image poetry* was coined in 1961, in connection with a kind of symbolist American poetry; it now is used to describe poetry that uses image to dip into the subconscious. Though not a label loved by everyone, the notion of the deep-image aesthetic is now as much part of the scholarly vocabulary as the tags of confessionalism, or Beat poetry.

However reductive, the label correctly identifies the centrality of image as a poetic tool. Bly's generation is famous for its renunciation of "craft" and the "technician's" approach to poetry. W. S. Merwin, Adrienne Rich, Allen Ginsberg—their insistence, in the sixties, that poetry was an act of spiritual necessity, a shamanic spiritual and political expression, fostered a sea change in American poetics. Good-bye New Criticism, good-bye careful irony and highly wrought detachment, good-bye academic specialists, good-bye, ultimately, reign of T. S. Eliot. In the sixties, for the second time in the twentieth century, American poets threw out formalisms and installed the image and the rhythm of breath as the fundamental agents of poetry.

García Lorca's "Little Infinite Poem" is one of the first poems offered in *Leaping Poetry*. Bly praises Lorca's passionate and hallucinatory imagery as the embodiment of the catapulting alternative consciousness:

> To take the wrong road
> is to arrive at the snow
> and to arrive at the snow
> is to get down on all fours for twenty centuries and eat the grasses
>   of the cemeteries.
>
> To take the wrong road
> is to arrive at woman,

woman who isn't afraid of light,
woman who kills two roosters in one second,
light which isn't afraid of roosters,
and roosters who don't know how to sing on top of the snow.

Lorca's lunging imagery, yoked to a subverted rhetoric of logic, intends to break the rational mind of the reader into an altered, archetype-rich state of consciousness. "When a poet creates a true image," says Bly, "he is gaining knowledge; he is bringing up into consciousness a connection that has been forgotten, perhaps for centuries. . . . The imagination calls on logic to help it create the true image and so to recover the forgotten relationship." Bly's contention is that images, with their cargo of irrational understanding, save poets and readers from the aridity of the analytical, mental willfulness, and certainty. It's not, Bly would say, that images overturn rationality; rather, images communicate the unsayable things they discover; images love rationality even as they erotically change its shape. "Lorca conveys his emotion not by any 'formula,'" says Bly, "but by means that do not occur to Eliot—by passion." Taking another dig at Eliot, Bly continues, "The phrase 'objective correlative' is astoundingly passionless. For Lorca there is no time to think of a cunning set of circumstances that would carry the emotion in a dehydrated form to which the reader need only add water."

In his advocacy of poetry from other traditions and cultures, Bly's assertion has been that, unlike cultures subjected to Western European Christian rationality, poets like Neruda and Lorca rediscovered the radical psychic freedom of the imagistic leap. Thus they can remind us how to get to a neglected part of the mind. For poets of the leaping image, says Bly, the poetic image is not a matter of vivifying equivalence, nor an expression of the poet's own personality, but an agent of deep truths of the soul, of the imagination:

Let's imagine a poem as if it were an animal. When animals run, they have considerable flowing rhythms. Also they have bodies. An image is simply a body where psychic energy is free to move around.

Such an emphasis is distinct from the Freudian model subscribed to by confessional poetry and therapeutic dream analysis, of "working things out," which sees adulthood as a fine-tuning of repression and compromise. Bly's love of radical poetic imagination for its own sake makes clear the difference between the aesthetics of deep image and concurrent practices of confessionalism, or the more extroverted orientations of say, Beat poetry or New York School poets. Bly, Wright, Merwin, and the other poets of that moment were invested in diving into the soul, into the collective unconscious; they were dowsing for spiritual truths that, although human, were more than an expression of one poet's individuality.

His Own Poetry

Bly's personal use of the image has undergone many permutations. His early poetry is fairly naturalistic. Images in his first book, *The Silence in the Snowy Fields* (1962), appeal in their plain, relaxed presentation. An atmosphere of solitude, privacy, and the intimacy of the self rules the book; the poems combine perceptions of nature, statement, and occasional touches of surrealism:

Driving to Town Late to Mail a Letter
It is a cold and snowy night. The main street is deserted.
The only things moving are swirls of snow.
As I lift the mailbox door, I feel its cold iron.
There is a privacy I love in this snowy night.
Driving around, I will waste more time.

Such unadornedness was completely fresh at that moment in American poetry; it modeled an unmannered and nonhysterical attention to inner life, to the natural world and the spiritual dimension of the self. This is a style not concerned with expressions of the poet's exceptional insight, but rather with registering qualities of innerness: stillness, longing, or unrest.

By 1968, and the publication of his second collection, *The Light around The Body,* Bly's image-making style had shifted. Bly's political and social focus had intensified: his new poems practiced a more radical and satiric surrealism. The ongoing political trespasses of national life seemed to elicit more and more radical imagery from poetry. The first stanza of "The Great Society" shows the kind of surrealism he was moving toward:

> Dentists continue to water their lawns even in the rain:
> Hands developed with terrible labor by apes
> Hang from the sleeves of evangelists;
> There are murdered kings in the light-bulbs outside movie
>   theaters:
> The coffins of the poor are hibernating in piles of new tires

The escalation of the Vietnam conflict escalated the anger and bewilderment of politicized American artists, including Bly, who played a central role in organizing readings around the country as part of American Writers Against the Vietnam War. Here is a passage from Bly's "Hatred of Men with Black Hair":

> We distrust every person on earth with black hair;
> We send teams to overthrow Chief Joseph's government;
> We train natives to kill Presidents with blowdarts;
> We have men loosening the nails on Noah's ark.
> ·
> . . . Underneath all the cement of the Pentagon
> There is a drop of Indian blood preserved in snow:
> Preserved from a trail of blood that once led away
> From the stockade, over the snow, the trail now lost.

The surrealist anger of Bly's images would reach its most extreme in *The Teeth Mother Naked at Last* (1970), a book-length hybrid of essay and poetry, linking archetypes, myth, contemporary politics, and poetry in a long hallucinatory poem responding to the historical hour. In *The Teeth Mother,* one feels the collaborating influence of Blake and Lorca:

Now the Chief Executive enters, and the press conference begins.
First the President lies about the date the Appalachian Mountains
   rose.
Then he lies about the population of Chicago, then he lies
   about the
            weight of the adult eagle, then about the acreage of the
               Everglades

He lies about the number of fish taken every year in the Arctic,
            he has private information about which city *is* the capital
            of Wyoming, he lies about the birthplace of Attila
            the Hun.

He lies about the composition of the amniotic fluid, and he insists
            that Luther never was a German, and that only the
            Protestants sold indulgences
            . . . .
And the Attorney General lies about the time the sun sets.

Of all the sides of Bly, perhaps this dark satirical ability has been the
least appreciated. Even in his most ferocious pronouncements there
is often something ribald and reckless in the language, which echoes
the savage hilarity of Blake's "Proverbs of Hell": "Prisons are built with
stones of Law, Brothels with bricks of Religion. . . . The tygers of wrath
are wiser than the horses of instruction. . . . Excess of sorrow laughs.
Excess of joy weeps. / The fox condemns the trap, not himself. / Joys
impregnate. Sorrows bring forth." In his early poems, one can see
Bly the poet building and amplifying his skill in the many dialects of
image. One can perceive, as well, another skill in the background—
the declarative voice of a natural didact and patriarch.

The Temptation to Bitterness: Politics plus Spirituality

Like many other poets of political engagement—Robinson Jeffers,
Philip Levine, Adrienne Rich, C. K. Williams, to name a few—Bly has

a streak of doomsday in his vision. If the world is offensive, imagining apocalypse is a tempting revenge upon it, and, like others, Bly has both raged and despaired. In *The Light around the Body,* and *The Teeth Mother Naked at Last,* the speaker frequently imagines a world ravaged by the death instinct of masculinity, or enthusiastically imagines the powerful overtaken by their own neglected spiritual lives, as in "The Busy Man Speaks":

> Not to the mother of solitude will I give myself
> Away, nor to the mother of love, nor to the mother of
>   conversation,
> Nor to the mother of art, nor the mother
> Of tears, nor the mother of the ocean;
> Not to the mother of sorrow, nor the mother
> Of the downcast face, nor the mother of the suffering of death;
> Not to the mother of the night full of crickets,
> Nor the mother of the open fields, nor the mother of Christ.
>
> But I will give myself to the father of righteousness, the father
> Of cheerfulness, who is also the father of rocks,
> Who is also the father of perfect gestures;
> From the Chase National Bank
> An arm of flame has come, and I am drawn
> To the desert, to the parched places, to the landscape of zeros;
> And I shall give myself away to the father of righteousness,
> The stones of cheerfulness, the steel of money, the father of rocks.

But apocalyptic fatalism carries with it certain dangers—grandiosity, morbidity, toxifying bitterness. In Bly's work, what has buffered the rage of self-righteousness, and dissipated its toxic pressure, is a framework larger than that of moral condemnation: the spiritual. Thus, though judgment is plentiful in his analysis of culture and human nature, the overall perspective one encounters in Bly's work is a diagnosis of spiritual sickness. History is a consequence of the failure of the spirit, and the breakdown of our mythic systems:

There is a wound on the trunk,
Where the branch was torn off.
A wind comes out of it,
Rising, swelling,
Swirling over everything alive.

("Melancholia")

The influence of Jungian thought, and of many other philosophical and mystic systems, runs pervasively through Bly's writing and thinking life. Thus, for all his social conscience, the epigraphs that litter Bly's first two books are not drawn from Marx, or Malcolm X, but from Jacob Boehme, the Swedish mystic:

When we think of it with this knowledge, we see that we have been locked up, and led blindfold, and it is the wise of this world who have shut up and locked us up in their art and their rationality, so that we have had to see with their eyes.

Images, images, images. The spiritual understructure of Bly's perspective has consistently retrieved the poet himself from bitterness. If life is mythically conceived of as a heroic journey, if the myth includes trials, errors, and failure as part of one's necessary education, it becomes less simple to focus blame outward upon one demonic enemy. Images can be found throughout Bly's work that ultimately direct the self toward the formation and reformation of vision; and one key factor in this vision is the acceptance and healing power of grief:

We did not come to remain whole.
We came to lose our leaves like the trees,
The trees that are broken
And start again, drawing up from the great roots;
Like mad poets captured by the Moors,
Men who live out
A second life.

("A Home in Dark Grass")

When, in 1968, *The Light around the Body* won the National Book Award, the recognition was not just aesthetic but political in import; at the public ceremony, Bly spoke against American foreign policy and, from the stage, signed over his prize money to a representative of the War Resisters League. In front of a large audience, he effectively committed a federal crime by encouraging the young man to burn his draft card. It was one of many acts Bly took as a prime mover of American Writers Against the Vietnam War, an alliance that gave readings and demonstrations around the country.

It is hard to identify the decisive moment when Robert Bly the poet became Robert Bly the cultural actor; yet it is clear that he had long felt the confinement of the conventional conception of the role of the "artist." Bly had been using his poems and critical essays to critique the American psyche from the start. He had applied Jungian theory to national identity and culture formation. His notions of Puritan hubris, masculine stoicism, and the anesthetic toxicity of materialism had been articulate from his first book. In one sense, generalizing his theories from the realm of American poetry to the culture at large was no great leap.

Yet when Bly the poet stepped over the professional perimeter that bounds the world of American poetry, his choice had consequences. It was a step that permanently separated Bly from the majority of his poetic peers. If, by stepping into the role of public intellectual, he had moved into a realm of higher or at least different stakes, from that time on, the world of the American arts academy would be essentially condescending toward Bly's own poems, and skeptical, often mocking, of his aspirations toward a larger field of influence than the aesthetic.

For his own part, even by age forty, Bly had resoundingly denounced the residence of poets inside universities; in Bly's view, universities, like most institutions, first co-opt writers as members of the middle class and then creatively desiccate them. They, in turn, deform their students with an overemphasis on technique and a deracination of the spiritual instinct. In "A Wrong Turning in American Poetry" and many other essays, Bly the critic dismisses a throng of poets, a list of names from the oughts to the sixties, for their poetic and spiritual shortcomings. Collectivity was one of those charges. For Bly, poetry is a free-range and solitary enterprise.

Meanwhile, Bly continued to invent and revise his own itinerary. A seminal moment arrived when Bly published *Iron John,* in 1990, a Jungian articulation, through fairy tales, of the stages of psychical masculine development. With the unexpected popularity of that book—it was on the *New York Times* best seller list for many weeks—some irrevocable corner was turned. The success of *Iron John* set in motion many forces. The way back was closed. From that time on, Bly's true companions would largely not be other American poets but cultural thinkers. On his alternative path, Bly's long association with psychologists, musicians, storytellers, and mythologists, including Joseph Campbell, James Hillman, and Marion Woodman, has played a role in his formation as influential as his relationships with scholars and poets.

Fast Forward

A comprehensive survey of all Bly's work is not possible here; there are simply too many phases of development to cover. However, a list of some of the poet's pursuits would include Bly's enthusiastic embrace of prose poems, for their virtue of "close looking." Likewise, Bly's editorship of many anthologies, including *The Soul Is Here for Its Own Joy* and the important *Rag and Bone Shop of the Heart,* has been a fundamental project. His substantial nonfiction meditation on American psychic immaturity, *The Sibling Society,* is a text that still seems urgently relevant today. And then there are Bly's extended explorations, in poetry and prose, of gender, mythology, and Eros.

This long development has been paralleled by the shifting currents of Bly's spiritual bearings, his changing field of vision, and his increasing attraction toward the ecstatic. The leaping and whirling ecstasis of imagistic energy was part of his poetic beginning, as was a steady emphasis upon the transcendental moment. However, reading Bly's work chronologically shows the poet's gradually growing affection for the ecstatic, non-Western traditions of Sufi, Persian, Arabian, and Indian devotional modes.

One way to read this attraction toward Eastern transcendental modes is to see it as Bly's avenue away from the psychic legacy of his Calvinist childhood and region. In Eastern poetry and philosophy Bly found a version of spiritual life that did not involve the puritanical notion of work as the only avenue to grace. Gradually, his preoccupation seems to have shifted from fighting battles with the world toward a more soul-centered metaphysics. This sea change, which seems to have been catalyzed by his translation of the Persian and Indian mystical poets, marked the beginning of a new stage in Bly's life and art.

The Limits

For all the energy and imagination of his poems, and for all the poet's admirable activities as cultural warrior, the main limitation in Bly's own poetry, it is generally conceded, is its lack of musicality. His natural talent for and emphasis upon the power of image have drawn him steadfastly toward values of plainspokenness and transparency of language. This preference is evident not just in his work but also in his translations, even of very musical poets like Rilke, whose work Bly translated into "American." It is also true of the American poets whose work he has most championed, such as Louis Simpson, David Ignatow, and William Stafford: all practitioners of a markedly plain style.

Another aspect of Bly's own art that has provoked critics is its intermittent awkwardness or goofiness—the odd, uneven image that seems plonked into the middle of an otherwise strong stanza or poem. In the name of intuition, he has, as a friend says, written his share of weird lines: "There is a joyful night in which we lose / Everything, and drift / like a radish" ("When the Dumb Speak"). Composed in spontaneity, there are plenty of moments that seem ungainly. "I stand without feathers on the shore / and watch the blood-colored moon gobbling up the sand." A friend of mine says such moments are, in their way, deliberate; Bly is not aiming at perfection but at a record of imaginative enactment. He chooses a reckless grandeur over the virtue of meticulousness.

Some of the stiffness of Bly's images arises, perhaps, from his long immersion in a different set of texts from the average American reader—not just translations but the antique idioms of fairy tale and myth, indigenous poetries and archetype analysis by Jungians. Images that might seem anachronistic to ordinary readers—dragons, for instance—may seem psychically vivacious to Bly, still alive in imaginative provenance. After all, two implications of the word *antique* are *valuable* and *obsolete*. "Toads nearby clap their small hands, and join / The fiery songs, their five long toes trembling in the soaked earth" ("Johnson's Cabinet Watched by Ants"). More recently, Bly's images are often drawn from the contexts of Sufi poetry; the conceits of the Beloved, the Garden, of the rose, and of wine may well be resonant in the pan-Arabic world, but not in American poetry.

The Ghazal: Image, Declaration, Paradox

Given his own mixed temperament of humor, wildness, and declaration, it seems right that Bly would eventually find his way to the ecstatic writing of the Sufis, the Urdu and Farsi poets of Persia and India. Starting with the poetry of Kabir and moving subsequently toward the ghazals of Rumi, Ghalib, and Hafez, these Eastern poetries have been among his major projects for the past thirty years. And, as will happen, Bly's vision, and his own poems, have been refreshed and reformed by his contact with Iranian poetics and poetry. In 1977, in *The Kabir Book*, Bly published his first Far East translations. Kabir has a bossy, slashing, humorous spirit, not unlike his translator's:

> I laugh when I hear that the fish in the water is thirsty.
>
> You don't grasp the fact that what is most alive of all
> is inside your own house;
> and so you walk from one holy city to the next with
> a confused look!
>
> Kabir will tell you the truth: go wherever you like,
> to Calcutta or Tibet;

if you can't find where your soul is hidden,
for you the world will never be real!

In the Indian poems of Kabir and Mirabai, Bly discovered not just a leaping poetry but a poetry of non-Western, devotional abandon, a spirit that disdains the fidgety cautions of the intellect. The devotional mode also contains another important modification of spiritual perspective: though it does not do away with responsibility, it essentially scoffs at the idea of the individual self, dignified by soul suffering. With its tropes of the divine teacher and the inner beloved, Sufism does away with the puritan notion of self-improvement as *work*; instead, it emphasizes the practices of longing, insight, and surrender:

> I said to the wanting-creature inside me:
> What is this river you want to cross?
> There are no travelers on the river-road, and no road.
> Do you see anyone moving about on that bank, or resting?
> There is no river at all, and no boat, and no boatman.
> There is no towrope either, and no one to pull it.
> There is no ground, no sky, no time, no bank, no ford!

On an intellectual level, and on the level of technique, these sharp-witted, ecstatic poets attuned Bly's mind to instincts that had been there all along—in particular a love of the liberating force of paradox, and the way in which crisscrossing lines of thought, images, and competing claims can be used poetically to pull apart the tight certainties of "knowing." Here are some couplets from Bly's translations of Hafez, from his anthology *The Soul Is Here For Its Own Joy: Sacred Poems from Many Cultures*. In the following poem, the repetition of one word, *turns,* morphs kaleidoscopically through context after context:

> The fire toward which we have turned our face is so intense
> It would set fire to the straw harvest of a hundred reasonable men.
>
> . . . .

From now on I will leave no doors in my heart open for love of
    beautiful creatures;
I have turned and set the seal of divine lips on the door of this
    house.

It's time to turn away from make-believe under our robes patched
    so many times.
The foundation for our work is an intelligence that sees though
    all these games.

We have turned our face to the pearl lying on the ocean floor.
So why then should we worry if this wobbly old boat keeps going
    or not?

We turn to the intellectuals and call them parasites of reason;
Thank God they are like true lovers faithless and without
    heart.

The Sufis have settled for a fantasy, and Hafez is no different.
How far out of reach our goals, and how weak our wills are!

The ghazal, as Hafez sings it, employs intellect as a form of *erotic*
play. "The Sufis have settled for a fantasy, and Hafez is no different."
The Eastern poets tutored Bly in a mode both non-Western and yet
intellectual, a poetics not dismissive of intellect, but capable of em-
bracing contradiction through a system of paradox and insight. For
Bly, the ghazal provided a sort of unified field theory of everything
he had learned and played with in the past. It offered him new poetic
configurations, forms that are both "leaping" and intellectually unified. It ultimately has resulted in a more integrative vision, one that
accommodates multiple flavors of fierceness, irony, and tenderness, as
in these tercets from one of Bly's own "American ghazals":

So many blessings have been given to us
During the first distribution of light, that we are
Admired in a thousand galaxies for our grief.

Don't expect us to appreciate creation or to
Avoid mistakes. Each of us is a latecomer
To the earth, picking up wood for the fire.

("Keeping Our Small Boat Afloat")

Seen from the Sufic spiritual perspective, the wastefulness of the human world is inevitable. The facts may be no less tragic than ever, but, since the world is a dance of the divine, the impulse to reform it becomes less desperate. The work of Hafez, with its combination of dazzling images and aphoristic discrimination, may have helped Bly unpack and resolve some of his own internal dualisms, in particular the split between ecstasy and intellect.

On a technical level, it is striking how the ghazal structure, both open and concentrated, also led Bly into the tightest poetic *form* he has ever written in: tercets in even-length lines, in which each self-sufficient tercet offers a new configuration or variation on a theme. Recurrence of the theme word is the stabilizing element, while a kaleidoscopic shifting of scale and focus from stanza to stanza both seduces the intellect and dissolves its attempts to cling. Under this influence, many of Bly's later poems manage to combine tragic and liberating visions, in a tone wealthy with experience, yet not overbearing in authority. A good example is "The Difficult Word" from *The Night Abraham Looked at the Stars* (2006). Like many ghazals, it is best presented in total to register the cumulative, complicating effect:

The oaks reluctantly let their leaves fall,
And hesitatingly allow their branches to be bare;
And the Bear spends all winter in separation.

The beauty of marriage is such that it dissolves
All earlier unions, and leads the man and wife
To walk together on the road of separation.

The word is a difficult one. The thought frightens us
That this planet with its darkening geese
Was created not for union but for separation.

Suppose there were a dragon curled inside each drop
Of water, defending its gold. It's possible
That abundance has the same effect as separation.

Each of us was glad floating in the loopy
Joy of the womb; but when our lips touched
Our mother's breast, we said, "This is separation."

It is my longing to smooth the feathers
Of birds and touch the hair of horses for hours
That has led me to spend my life in separation.

Plain enough in its language, tercet by tercet "The Difficult Word" may seem initially simple. Its cumulative impact, though, resides in the orbital, rotating strategy of the ghazal, in which each tercet displaces and sometimes contradicts the one before, and at the same time extends the thematic substance of the poem. Thus, a ghazal gathers more meaning and poignancy than many more obviously sophisticated poems. "The Difficult Word" rotates through contexts of nature, marriage, infancy, fate, affluence, and communion; with its play of tones, and its mixed messages, it has the quality of good news, bad news joke. As Hafez says:

In the five days remaining to you in this rest stop
Before you go to the grave, take it easy, give
Yourself time, because time is not all that great.

The ghazal, even in its adopted American form, is radical in its refusal of linearity and traditional logic. Yet it has provided a very American poet, Bly, with access to a freshly unsentimental and integrated vision. Without forgetting the social realities of human life, Bly's own late work still insists upon the actuality of the transcendental, and the central importance of what Keats called soul-making.

Conclusion

In his lifetime Robert Bly has introduced more energy, ideas, and technique into American poetry than can be measured. In a different America, or in an era in which politics, art, and spirituality were not segregated, Bly would have been a natural pick for U.S. poet laureate. It can be safely presumed that he was always too political and too impetuous. In our era, his stature might accurately be compared to that of Studs Terkel, Cornel West, or Susan Sontag—a public intellectual. Beginning from the marginalized position of American poet, he took upon himself the task of reading and explaining the world to citizens, while at the same time asserting viable and visionary countervalues. Though Bly's lens for such work has primarily been poetry, his enterprise has not been confined to art salons and universities. Only a few individuals in American poetry seem comparable, in longevity and energy, as bridge builders and identity creators: Pound, Snyder, Ginsberg, and Rich come to mind.

It may be as a maker of communities, literal and virtual, that Bly has made some of his greatest contributions. Bringing American readers into intimate contact with European and Eastern poetries has irrevocably enlarged the scale of our literate worlds. Many long-running American colloquia and conferences—the men's movement, the war resisters, the Rumi lovers, the Conference on the Great Mother and New Father, each one distinct from the others—owe their continuing existence to Bly's charisma and exertion.

Nonetheless, troubling afterthoughts arise from considering Bly's career as an era. What, after all, we might ask, has changed in the condition of American citizens? The U.S. government is now involved in multiple conflicts in the Middle East and Africa; American citizens are more economically polarized than ever, and are manipulated by ever-more sophisticated, pervasive forces of media and consumerism. Everywhere one looks one sees human beings with heads bent, focused on hand-held phones, computers, and other devices. Thanks to technology, awareness is more far-reaching and yet narrower than ever. It is richer in potential and yet ever more degraded in practice.

As Rilke would say, we reach for everything and grasp nothing. It is not a hopeful scene. Nor are the adversaries of conscience and consciousness as easy to name and define as they were fifty years ago; the sources of oppression can no longer accurately be labeled as patriarchy, J. P. Morgan, or IBM. Lacking an enemy with a location, we find more difficulty than ever in formulating countervalues. Our contemporary "civilized" condition more resembles the stormy, bewildered realms painted by William Blake and Hieronymus Bosch. Meanwhile, contemporary American poetry seems less political and more esoterically self-involved than ever.

Against this background, the scale and variety of Bly's poetic career are inspirational and sobering. The account recorded here is not the half of it—his has been a life of many selves, poems, and frontiers, many mistakes and successes. His fearless opposition to the soul-killing aspects of American history and culture, his work as an ambassador of poetry, and his great curiosity and impetuousness as an advocate of consciousness-raising have resulted in great achievements. One can only wonder, where will we find another like him?

◇ ◇ ◇ ◇ ◇

Twenty Poems That Could Save America

What went wrong? Somehow, we blew it. We never quite got poetry inside the American school system and thus never quite inside the culture. Many brave people have tried, tried for decades, are surely still trying. The most recent watermark of their success was the introduction of Robert Frost and Carl Sandburg and some E. E. Cummings, of "The Love Song of J. Alfred Prufrock" and "In a Station of the Metro"—this last poem ponderously explained, but at least clean and classical, as quick as an inoculation. It isn't really fair to blame contemporary indifference to poetry on "The Emperor of Ice-Cream." Nor is it fair to blame Wallace Stevens himself, who also left us, after all, "Thirteen Ways of Looking at a Blackbird," a poem that will continue to electrify and intrigue far more curious young minds than are anesthetized by a bad day of pedagogy on the ice cream poem. Let us blame instead the stuffed shirts who took an hour to explain that poem in their classrooms, who chose it because it would *need* an explainer; pretentious ponderous ponderosas of professional professors will always be drawn to the poems that require a priest.

Still, we have failed. The fierce life force of contemporary American poetry never made it through the metal detector of the public school system. In the seventies, our hopes seemed justified; those Simon and Garfunkel lyrics were being mimeographed and discussed by the skinny teacher with the sideburns, Mr. Ogilvy, who was dating the teacher with the miniskirt and the Joan Baez LPs ("Students, you can call me Brenda"). Armed with the poems of Lawrence Ferlinghetti and Richard Brautigan, fifteen-year-olds were writing their first Jim Morrison lyrics, their Kerouacian chants to existential night.

But it never took. We flunked.

Sure, there would always be those rare kids who got it anyway; who *got,* really *got* "I have given my heart away, a sordid boon!," got it because they were old souls, preternaturally, precociously alert to the pitfalls of grown-up life, the legion opportunities for self-betrayal, the army of counterfeit values surrounding them. They were the ones who memorized "Dover Beach" and throatily recited it to their sweethearts in the backseat of a Chevrolet on the night of junior prom, and then once more for select friends at the afterparty.

Nonetheless, it is common knowledge: real live American poetry is absent from our public schools. The teaching of poetry languishes, and that region of youthful neurological terrain capable of being ignited and aria'd only by poetry is largely dark, unpopulated, and silent, like a classroom whose door is unopened, whose shades are drawn.

This is more than a shame, for poetry is our common treasure-house, and we need its aliveness, its respect for the subconscious, its willingness to entertain ambiguity; we need its plaintive truth telling about the human condition and its imaginative exhibitions of linguistic freedom, which confront the general culture's more grotesque manipulations. We need the emotional training sessions poetry conducts us through. We need its previews of coming attractions: heartbreak, survival, failure, endurance, understanding, more heartbreak.

I have met, over the years, many remarkable English teachers who make poetry vivid and real to their students—but they are the exception. By far the majority of language arts teachers feel lost when it comes to poetry. They themselves were never initiated into its freshness and vitality. Thus they lack not only confidence in their ability to teach poetry but also confidence in their ability to *read* poetry! And, unsurprisingly, they don't know which poems to teach.

The first part of the fix is very simple: the list of poems taught in our schools needs to be updated. We must make a new and living catalog accessible to teachers as well as students. The old chestnuts— "The Road Not Taken," "I Heard a Fly Buzz When I Died," "Do Not

Go Gentle into That Good Night," great, worthy poems all—must be removed and replaced by poems that are not chestnuts. This refreshing of canonical content and tone will vitalize teachers and students everywhere, and just may revive our sense of the currency and relevance of poetry. Accomplish that, and we can renew the conversation, the teaching, everything.

But, I hear some protest, aren't the old poems good enough? Aren't great poems enduring in their worth and perennial in their appeal? Love, death, strife, joy, loneliness—aren't these the recurrent, always-relevant subject matter of our shared songs? In catering to the contemporary, wouldn't we be lowering the caliber of the art we present to our youth? Isn't this a capitulation to a superficial culture and the era of disposability?

Such questions are beside the point, since poetry is *not* being transmitted from one generation to the next. The cultural chain has been broken, as anyone paying attention knows. Moreover, the written word always needs renewal. Art must be recast continually. "Dover Beach" and "My Mistress' Eyes Are Nothing Like the Sun" are not lost, but instead are being rewritten again and again, a hundred times for each new generation.

If anthologies were structured to represent the way that most of us actually learn, they would begin in the present and "progress" into the past. I read Lawrence Ferlinghetti before I read D. H. Lawrence before I read Thomas Wyatt. Once the literate appetite is whetted, it will keep turning to new tastes. A reader who first falls in love with Billy Collins or Mary Oliver is likely then to drift into an anthology that includes Emily Dickinson and Thomas Hardy.

The second part of the fix is rather more complicated: in addition to rebooting the American poetic canon as a whole, we must establish a kind of national core curriculum, a set of poems held in common by our students and so by our citizens. In the spirit of boosterism, I have selected twenty works I believe worthy of inclusion in this curriculum—works I believe could empower us with a common vocabulary of stories, values, points of reference. The brief explications and justifications I offer below for ten of these poems are not meant to foreclose the interpretive possibilities that are part of a good poem's life force. Rather, I hope they will suggest areas worthy of more cultivation in that mysterious inner space, the American mind.

Poetry Teaches the Ethical Nature of Choice

To visualize this poetry-enriched near future, please imagine that somewhere in the echoey, high-ceilinged meeting rooms of our nation's Capitol, a congressional committee is in session. It is midsummer in Washington, D.C., and a pitcher of water is on the table, beads of condensation on its side; the ice has melted. A difficult bill is also on the table, one in which the exigencies of the political present must be weighed against the needs of the future; say, for example, that the subsidized production of corn for ethanol might be given priority over other alternatives to gasoline. Too many midwestern farmers have become dependent on these subsidies. But if policy is changed now, they will suffer.

"It's like that William Stafford poem," says one congressional aide. "What's the title—the one about the deer?"

"'Traveling through the Dark,'" says a representative from Kansas. The poem begins:

> Traveling through the dark I found a deer
> dead on the edge of the Wilson River road.
> It is usually best to roll them into the canyon:
> that road is narrow; to swerve might make more dead.

"That's the one," says the aide. "Yeah, that scene where the guy has to decide whether to push the mother deer over the edge of the cliff to make the road safer—even though the deer is pregnant, with a fawn inside her."

"'To swerve might make more dead,'" says someone else.

"Yes," says the first legislator. "Here we are, getting ready to choose some lives over others, to clear the road for traffic. Are we going to push the deer over the side of the highway?"

"When you put it like that," says another, "I think we should wait."

"That's not deciding," says a third congressman. "That's procrastinating. I say we vote right now."

. . . Beside that mountain road I hesitated.

The car aimed ahead its lowered parking lights;
under the hood purred the steady engine.
I stood in the glare of the warm exhaust turning red;
around our group I could hear the wilderness listen.

I thought hard for us all—my only swerving—,
then pushed her over the edge into the river.

"Traveling through the Dark" is a well-known poem, but one with legs yet—it offers a lucid ethical dilemma that foregrounds the nature of moral choice.

Poetry Respects Solitude and Self-Discovery

Here's another scenario. A woman, recently divorced from her husband of twenty-five years (he fell in love with his yoga instructor). Living in the city where they shared a life together, she's discovering what it's like to be single at fifty. She has a busy professional life and can handle the daylight hours, but the nights are hard, and she's decided she'd better stay away from wine in the evening. She believes she might be alone for the rest of her days.

One night on the train home, she remembers a poem from tenth grade called "Bamboo and a Bird." When she gets back to her apartment, she looks it up on the Internet. It's by Linda Gregg:

In the subway late at night.
Waiting for the downtown train
at Forty-Second Street.
Walking back and forth
on the platform.

Too tired to give money.
Staring at the magazine covers
in the kiosk. Someone passes me
from behind, wearing an orange vest
and dragging a black hose.
A car stops and the doors open.
All the faces are plain.
It makes me happy to be
among these people
who leave empty seats
between each other.

Reading the poem, the divorcée finds focus. "It reminded me," she says to her friend the following week, "that there can be dignity in being alone. Remember the woman in the poem? She sees everything so clearly *because* she's alone."

"Yes," says the friend. "She has this pride about being alone."

"No, it's not pride, exactly—she just *sees* what is in front of her. Because she's tired. She can see because she's exhausted and by herself. And even though those other people are maybe unhappy and poor, like her, she isn't responsible for them. They don't need to be changed. They can't change. All of them, they just are what they are."

"No shame, no pity."

"It's all right to be lonely, because everyone else is, too. There's company in loneliness." She pauses.

"It's like existentialism with a hand warmer."

"What about that guy in the poem, who goes past, pulling the hose? We could never figure that out in class."

"I don't know what that hose is about. Does everything have to represent something?"

Poetry Stimulates Daring

At this point, perhaps, you may feel you are on the receiving end of a William Bennett–style sermon on Poetry as Moral Improvement.

That intuition is only partially right. Not all of the twenty poems I've selected have "instruction" as their agenda. Their usefulness is not so constrained or predictable. Poems are existentially unconventional: though some may look like philosophical fitness equipment, designed for self-improvement, others may look like Siamese cats. Consider, as an example of something unpredictable, the following poem by Kerry Johannsen:

> **Black People & White People Were Said**
> to disappear if we looked at
> each other too long
> especially the young ones—
> especially growing boys & girls
>
> the length of a gaze was
> watched sidewise
> as a kingsnake
> eyeing a copperhead while hands
> of mothers and fathers gently
> tugged their children close
>
> white people & black people were said to
> disappear if but nobody ever said it
> loud nobody said it
> at all & nobody ever
> talked about where
> the ones who didn't listen
> went

Johannsen's poem helps us to name a feature of the social land-scape that every American will recognize; it drags into plain sight, and into our common vision, the mystery of race and the ominous way it plays out in our collective social life. It describes the haunted con-dition that results from repressed knowledge. Moreover, Johannsen's poem does not avoid complexity in order to create agreement. It does not accuse or judge or cry out; it speaks from the position neither of the oppressor nor of the victim. The poem's vocal tone is largely one of wonder, which makes it an unthreatening place to begin a conversation about a touchy subject.

Alarmed by the rapid erosion of shared knowledge among Americans, the liberal scholar E. D. Hirsch took on the role of cultural correctionist with his best-selling book, *Cultural Literacy* (1987). Hirsch argued that, without the propagation of a common vocabulary— Benedict Arnold, Sigmund Freud, *King Lear,* "revenuers," the Cold War, Emmett Till, gerrymandering—the American cultural fabric would fray and fall apart. Indeed, unless we continue to renew and supplement our common intellectual property, we can and will get stupider, less comprehending of one another, more disconnected.

The scaffoldings of cultural identity can be either trivial or profound, toxic or sustaining, ephemeral or lasting. The celebrity culture that seems ubiquitous in our moment is a kind of fake surrogate for the culturally significant place gods and myth once held in the collective imagination. The sagas of Princess Di, or Michael Jackson, or Amy Winehouse are shallow substitutes for the story of Persephone, lacking the structure to edify but charismatic to many people nonetheless. Just as junk food mimics nutritious food, fake culture mimics and displaces real myth. Real culture cultivates our ability to see, feel, and think. It is empowering. Fake culture renders us passive, materialistic, and tranced-out.

Culturally important artworks establish new benchmarks of relevance, break icons, embody new recognitions for a people and a time. "Diving into the Wreck," *Citizen Kane,* "Prufrock," *Glengarry Glen Ross.* In poetry, as in other art forms, some works are of significance for cultural reasons, some for aesthetic. Both categories are legitimate, and, of course, they sometimes overlap. Artworks may sometimes lose their shape and resonance, their intensity and relevance, in five years, or ten, or fifty—and what's wrong with that? The relative value of the "immortal" and the "contemporary" has been the subject of many intellectual battles, but why can't these categories coexist?

The idealized America envisioned by Hirsch—one shored up by the deliberate revival of old and new traditions—would be one in which poems were part of the civility and pleasure of the dining table, in which guests and hosts staged impromptu readings, in which poems could usefully and naturally be worked into a conversation about anything at all. Is such a culture so far from possible?

Poetry Rehabilitates Language

Muriel Rukeyser's "The Ballad of Orange and Grape" can teach us something about the fundamental import of language. Charming and didactic, the poem asks what it means when language is allowed to be unreliable. What, it wonders, happens to culture then?

> After you finish your work
> after you do your day
> after you've read your reading
> after you've written your say—
> you go down the street to the hot dog stand,
> one block down and across the way.
> On a blistering afternoon in East Harlem in the twentieth century.
> . . . .
>   Frankfurters, frankfurters sizzle on the steel
> where the hot-dog-man leans—
> nothing else on the counter
> but the usual two machines,
> the grape one, empty, and the orange one, empty,
> I face him in between.
> A black boy comes along, looks at the hot dogs, goes on walking.
>
> I watch the man as he stands and pours
> in the familiar shape
> bright purple in the one marked ORANGE
> orange in the one marked GRAPE,
> the grape drink in the machine marked ORANGE
> and orange drink in the GRAPE.
> Just the one word large and clear, unmistakable, on each machine.

I ask him: How can we go on reading
and make sense out of what we read?—
How can they write and believe what they're writing,
the young ones across the street,
while you go on pouring grape into ORANGE
and orange into the one marked GRAPE—? . . .

He looks at the two machines and he smiles
and he shrugs and smiles and pours again.
It could be violence and nonviolence
it could be black and white, women and men
it could be war and peace or any
binary system, love and hate, enemy, friend.
Yes and no, be and not-be, what we do and what we don't do.

On a corner in East Harlem
garbage, reading, a deep smile, rape,
forgetfulness, a hot street of murder,
misery, withered hope,
a man keeps pouring grape into ORANGE
and orange into the one marked GRAPE,
pouring orange into GRAPE and grape into ORANGE forever.

Rukeyser's overt educational intention here may evoke a reflex uneasiness among some poetry lovers. When a work of art aims directly
at "the public welfare," the first objection concerns the proper motive
of art. What is it art for? Beauty or truth? Entertainment or character
building? Is painting *X* worth looking at because of its subtle color, its
ugliness, its idealism, its truth telling, or because of its conversation
with the history of aesthetics? Is the essence of art the unique expression of individuality, or of a cultural condition? When art is evaluated
or loved for its "utility," its ethical benefits, artists and intellectuals
object that it has been demeaned, commodified, and oversimplified.
The civic bureaucracy, meanwhile, argues that art is just not verifi-
able *enough* in its beneficence. But if we said that elementary school

playgrounds, with their monkey bars and swing sets, were intended to build hand-eye coordination and balance, would that make playgrounds oppressive or less fun?

Rukeyser's poem delivers its crucial idea in brief and forceful form, and although poems need no instructional end point to justify themselves, hers accomplishes its mission memorably. The American who has read it will never take as a given the duplicitous, inaccurate language that surrounds us commercially and politically in the way that Rukeyser's speaker does. She urges us instead to see the corruption of language as it should be seen: as an ethical betrayal, as nothing less than an existential insult, one with snowballing consequences. Orange for grape, grape for orange—such a commonplace misrepresentation may seem trivial alongside fibs about weapons of mass destruction, yet it can lead into the valleys and mountains of bad faith. "The Ballad of Orange and Grape" provides anyone who has encountered it with a correlative, a reference point by which to recognize how certain worldly forces (in this case, indifference) anesthetize our language and thereby steal our reality.

Obviously, poems in a curriculum may usefully complicate and contradict one another.

"The Ballad of Orange and Grape" addresses the ethics of language and the need for trustworthy speech. Against Rukeyser's urgent formulation of that truth, one might, in our imaginary curriculum, counterpose Walt Whitman's "When I Heard the Learn'd Astronomer," which asserts the superiority of silence and nature to scholarly language and ideas. In Whitman's poem, two kinds of learning are opposed to each other, and the speaker advocates playing hooky:

> When I heard the learn'd astronomer;
> When the proofs, the figures, were ranged in columns before me;
> When I was shown the charts and the diagrams, to add, divide,
>   and measure them;
> When I, sitting, heard the astronomer, where he lectured with
>   much applause in the lecture-room,
> How soon, unaccountable, I became tired and sick;

Till rising and gliding out, I wander'd off by myself,
In the mystical moist night-air, and from time to time,
Look'd up in perfect silence at the stars.

"When I Heard the Learn'd Astronomer" represents a streak of anti-intellectualism that is a familiar part of the American tradition of self-sufficiency and independence. The natural man, claims the poem, has little need for arid recitations of classroom knowledge. Rather, as Emerson suggested, it is the true work of each American to go outside and forge her own original relationship with the universe. Whitman's lyric embodies that American narrative.

Is it so hard to believe that only twenty poems, commonly possessed and mutually valued, could make a difference in American culture? Our skepticism is founded in our ingrained impression of poetry as anemic, difficult, and obscure. We believe that, like other kinds of "high" art, poems must be force-fed to people; that poems are prissy, refined, cerebral, rhymed; that they are a kind of test devised to separate the bumpkins from the aesthetes. At bottom, such a prejudice, pervasive as it is, imagines that culture is a side dish to the meal of economic realism, an innocuous auxiliary to our lives.

To underestimate the appeal of art is to underestimate not only poetry but also human nature. Our hunger for myth, story, and design is very deep. I hold these poems' truths to be self-evident. If we are not in love with poems, the problem may be that we are not teaching the right poems. Yet ignorance of and wariness about art gets passed on virally, from teacher to student. After a few generations of such exile, poetry will come to be viewed as a stuffy neighborhood of large houses with locked doors, where no one wants to spend any time.

Poetry Defuses Sexual Anxiety and Encourages Curiosity

Sharon Olds's "Topography" could perhaps shatter the petrified classroom notion that poetry has no libido or sense of humor. The poem's narrative achievement is to be both playful and wholesome on the subject of sex. "Topography" is also a tutorial in the pleasures of extended metaphor and language itself, allowed as it is to somersault in a nondirective, extracurricular capacity:

> After we flew across the country we
> got into bed, laid our bodies
> delicately together, like maps laid
> face to face, East to West, my
> San Francisco against your New York, your
> Fire Island against my Sonoma, my
> New Orleans deep in your Texas, your Idaho
> bright on my Great Lakes, my Kansas
> burning against your Kansas your Kansas
> burning against my Kansas, your Eastern
> Standard Time pressing into my
> Pacific Time, my Mountain Time
> beating against your Central Time, your
> sun rising swiftly from the right my
> sun rising swiftly from the left your
> moon rising slowly from the left my
> moon rising slowly from the right until
> all four bodies of the sky
> burn above us, sealing us together,
> all our cities twin cities,
> all our states united, one
> nation, indivisible, with liberty and justice for all.

The former U.S. poet laureate Robert Pinsky once said that American poetry would be a warmer, more inviting place if it included more sex, humor, and violence—if, in some ways, it artfully incorporated some of the "life-affirming vulgarity" of the popular entertainment that has, it sometimes seems, elbowed it aside. Olds's poem dispels the atmosphere of stodginess and elitism we culture lovers must constantly resist. It also sets the table for a host of subsidiary conversations on subjects ranging from patriotism to porn, from the curious pleasure of phonemes ("Sonoma") to the nature of innuendo ("Fire

Island"). The god of play is Eros, and sometimes art leads with the libido. If Americans only knew that poetry is sexy, surely more books would be checked out of the library. "Topography" demonstrates one of the wondrous facts of American poetry—its populist brilliance and range. It can be high and low, entertaining, erudite, provocative, rude, brainy, and mysterious.

Poems Acknowledge Trouble Ahead

Gender is such an inextricable part of our lives and our identities, it is safe to say we will spend our lives trying to untangle its truths and mysteries. The literature of gender is vast because the struggle to understand is a fundamental one; yet the incisive swiftness of poetry cuts to the heart of most subjects, including this one. Whereas "Topography" praises the united states of sex, the inevitable difficulties between male and female are addressed more seriously in "A Man and a Woman," by Alan Feldman. In fierce, fast-moving, broken-off lines, the poem catalogs the passionate suspicions and doubts of each gender toward the other. Feldman's poem opens door after door for discussion, and closes none of them:

> Between a man and a woman
> the anger is greater, for each man would like to sleep
> in the arms of each woman,
> who would like to sleep in the arms
> of each man, if she trusted him not to be
> schizophrenic, if he trusted her
> not to be a hypochondriac,
> if she trusted him not to leave her
> too soon, if he trusted her not to
> hold him too long,
> and often women stare at the word *men*
> as it lives in the word *women*,
> as if each woman
> carried a man inside her and a woe,

and has crying fits that last for days,
not like the crying of a man,
which lasts a few seconds, and rips
the throat like a claw—
but because the pain differs
much as the shape of the body,
the woman takes the suffering of the man
for selfishness, the man the woman's pain
for helplessness, the woman's lack
of it for hardness, the man's tenderness
an act of contempt,
which is really fear,
the man's fear for fickleness . . .
Yet cars come off the bridge in rivers of light,
each holding a man and a woman.

The difficulties and differences are immense—"Yet cars come off the bridge in rivers of light / each holding a man and a woman." Feldman's poem is tough, true, and vivid enough to deserve registration in our communal anthology. It begins, artfully, with a declared but never explicitly answered question. The anger between the man and the woman is "greater" than *what?* Love? Greater than the other sorts of anger we feel? The way this opening grammar hangs, semantically incomplete, is one of the poem's many charms and sophistications. The catalog of gendered differences, clearly compiled from experience in the field, is a provocative pleasure of its own. It is not hard to imagine the difference this poem might make in helping a husband and wife to consider the reasons for tolerance.

Poems Rehearse the Future

Poems, some more than others, are songs, passed down through time. It is amazing how far and how long they can travel and still remain fresh. Was there ever a poet named Speaks-Fluently? That is the name assigned to the author of this Native American poem of Osage origin, passed on to me by another poet. "Song of Speaks-Fluently" is as light as a nursery rhyme and as serious as a gospel; wry, yet firm about the facts of life. And what a flavor of reliability it bears from its at once distant and personal source.

> To have to carry your own corn far—
> who likes it?
> To follow the black bear through the thicket—
> who likes it?
> To hunt without profit, to return weary without anything—
> who likes it?
> You have to carry your own corn far.
> You have to follow the black bear.
> You have to hunt to no profit.
>
> If not, what will you tell the little ones? What will you speak of?
> For it is bad not to use the talk which God has sent us.
> I am Speaks-Fluently. Of all the groups of symbols,
> I am a symbol by myself.
>
> Trans. Mary Ruefle

Here is the news, says the poem sympathetically: you too shall labor, and on Tuesday your enterprise shall not succeed, and on Wednesday you shall bend again to the labor before you. Now, this is a message well worth inclusion in the speech of any high school valedictorian in America. Instead of demanding favors of the universe, Speaks-Fluently tells us, we must cultivate the wisdom of the shrug and exercise the muscle of persistence. "You have to carry your own corn far. . . . You have to hunt to no profit."

With its images of ancient farming and hunting, "Song of Speaks-Fluently" carries another quiet implication—that we readers, whatever our work, are connected to the oldest rhythms of human effort and human survival. The necessities and hazards of our lives have changed in appearance, but not in essence.

A thousand kinds of poems exist, and they point in an infinite number of directions.

Poems Teach Aesthetics That Are of Broad Application

Another dividend of even a basic investment in poetry is the way it refines our sensitivity for tone, for subtleties of inflection, which in turn enables us to navigate the world more skillfully. Take the delicate, tentative mix of irony and affection in "The Geraniums," by Genevieve Taggard:

> Even if the geraniums are artificial,
> Just the same
> In the rear of the Italian cafe
> Under the nimbus of electric light
> They are red, no less red
> For how they were made. Above
> The mirror and the napkins
> In the little white pots . . .
> . . . In the semi-clean cafe
> Where they have good
> Lasagna . . . the red is a wonderful joy
> Really, and so are the people
> Who like and ignore it. In this place
> They also have good bread.

Taggard's poem, delivered in a reflective, tender, meditative voice, is about aesthetics. It asks an interesting question: Can a thing be simultaneously false and beautiful? Is the modern world, with its manifold illusions, nonetheless an environment in which the soul can find nourishment? What do we see and what do we habitually ignore? Can we train ourselves to appreciate *any* environment? Consider the loveliness of the humble fake flowers! To cultivate an ear for tone is, oddly enough, to cultivate one's own perceptual alertness. In "The

Geraniums," irony and wonder (the "semi-clean cafe" and the "wonder-ful joy really" of red) collaborate intricately in the speaker's casually unfolding voice. To develop an ear for such delicate modulations is in fact a survival skill useful for a lifetime.

I could go on with more examples. My list is ready—I am only wait-ing for the president to give me the go-ahead. Perhaps twenty other experienced readers of poetry might come up with twenty other lists of poems that might similarly serve, poems that could be smuggled into twenty-first-century life as amulets and beatitudes to guide, map, empower, and console. The argument of this essay is not complex; the poems are richly so.

Poems build our capacity for imaginative thinking, create a toler-ance for ambiguity, and foster an appreciation for the role of the un-known in human life. From such compact structures of language, from so few poems, so much can be reinforced that is currently at risk in our culture. As an American writer, I long for the art form to be restored to its position in culture, one of relevance and utility, to do what it can. In everything we have to understand, poems can help.

To implement a program of poetry reading and appreciation across the educational system, in prep schools and charter schools as well as in public schools, would take daring and conviction and willing-ness. It would take the willingness of teachers to enjoy poems them-selves, to handle a kind of material that aims not to quantify, define, or test but to open one door after another down a long hallway. To communicate credulity requires credulity, the faith that a small good thing contains the potential for great transformations. Yet our own lives provide the testimony that futures are formed from such chance encounters, such small receptions and affections. In increment after increment, the grace of the future depends on the preparation and generosity of the past. It is that incidental, almost accidental, encoun-ter with memorable beauty or knowledge—that news that comes from poetry—that enables us, as the poem by William Stafford says, to think hard for us all.

Twenty Poems That Could Save America

"Twenty-First. Night. Monday," by Anna Akhmatova

"God's Justice," by Anne Carson

"memory," by Lucille Clifton

"A Man and a Woman," by Alan Feldman

"America," by Allen Ginsberg

"Bamboo and a Bird," by Linda Gregg

"The Sick Child," by Randall Jarrell

"Black People & White People Were Said," by Kerry Johannsen

"Topography," by Sharon Olds

"Wild Geese," by Mary Oliver

"Written in Pencil in the Sealed Railway Car," by Dan Pagis

"Merengue," by Mary Ruefle

"The Ballad of Orange and Grape," by Muriel Rukeyser

"Waiting for Icarus," by Muriel Rukeyser

"American Classic," by Louis Simpson

"Song of Speaks-Fluently," by Speaks-Fluently

"Traveling through the Dark," by William Stafford

"The Geraniums," by Genevieve Taggard

"When I Heard the Learn'd Astronomer," by Walt Whitman

"Our Dust," by C. D. Wright

ACKNOWLEDGMENTS

Many thanks to the editors and publications in which these essays have previously appeared, sometimes in different versions. I also want to thank my most faithful, recurrent, and meticulous readers of these essays in draft form, Carl Dennis and Kathleen Lee. Peter Harris's insights about poetry were repeatedly valuable. And many thanks to editor Jeff Shotts, for his painstaking and helpful scrutiny of all these essays. A conversation with Rob Casper was responsible for the title essay.

The American Poetry Review: "'Regard the Twists of the Bugle / That Yield One Clear Clarion': The Dean Young Effect"; "Unarrestable: The Poetic Development of Sharon Olds"; "Soul Radio: Marie Howe, Jane Hirshfield, and Linda Gregg"; "The Village Troublemaker: Robert Bly and American Poetry"

Gulf Coast: "Litany, Game, and Representation: Charting the Course from the Old to the New Poetry"

Harper's (online): "Twenty Poems That Could Save America"

The Kenyon Review: "Idiom, Our Funny Valentine"

Poetry: "Vertigo, Recognition, and Passionate Worldliness"

The Writer's Chronicle: "*Je Suis ein Americano:* The Genius of American Diction"; "Poetic Housing: Shifting Parts and Changing Wholes"; "'I Do This, I Do That': The Strange Legacy of New York School Poetics"

TONY HOAGLAND has published four collections of poems, including *Unincorporated Persons in the Late Honda Dynasty* and *What Narcissism Means to Me,* a finalist for the National Book Critics Circle Award. He is also the author of a previous book of essays, *Real Sofistikashun: Essays on Poetry and Craft.* He has received the Jackson Poetry Prize from *Poets & Writers,* the O. B. Hardison Award for teaching from the Folger Shakespeare Library, and the Mark Twain Award for humor in American poetry from the Poetry Foundation, as well as fellowships from the National Endowment for the Arts and the Guggenheim Foundation. In 2011, Hoagland started Five Powers Poetry, a program to coach teachers in the teaching of poetry in the classroom. He teaches at the University of Houston and in the Warren Wilson College MFA program.

Twenty Poems That Could Save America is set in Arno Pro, a face designed by Robert Slimbach and named after the river that runs through Florence. Book design by Ann Sudmeier. Composition by BookMobile Design & Digital Publisher Services, Minneapolis, Minnesota. Manufactured by Versa Press on acid-free 30 percent postconsumer wastepaper.